tiny plants

Brimming with creative inspiration, how-to projects, and useful information to enrich your everyday life, Quarto Knows is a favorite destination for those pursuing their interests and passions. Visit our site and dig deeper with our books into your area of interest: Quarto Creates, Quarto Cooks, Quarto Homes, Quarto Lives, Quarto Drives, Quarto Explores, Quarto Gifts, or Quarto Kids.

© 2021 Quarto Publishing Group USA Inc.
Text © 2021 Leslie F. Halleck

First Published in 2021 by Cool Springs Press, an imprint of The Quarto Group, 100 Cummings Center, Suite 265-D, Beverly, MA 01915, USA.
T (978) 282-9590 F (978) 283-2742
QuartoKnows.com

Cool Springs Press titles are also available at discount for retail, wholesale, promotional, and bulk purchase. For details, contact the Special Sales Manager by email at specialsales@quarto.com or by mail at The Quarto Group, Attn: Special Sales Manager, 100 Cummings Center, Suite 265-D, Beverly, MA 01915, USA.

ISBN: 978-0-7603-6957-9

Digital edition published in 2021
eISBN: 978-0-7603-6958-6

Library of Congress Cataloging-in-Publication Data is available.

Design and page layout: Laura Shaw Design
Photography: Leslie F. Halleck except for: Blooming Tables, page 165 all; Gardener's Supply, page 53 all; Lisa Eldred Steinkopf, page 88; Lise Lefebvre, Botanopia, page 162 right and page 167 right; Orchidarium, LLC, page 29; Shutterstock, pages 16, 26, 28 top, 29 left, and 30; Soiltech Solutions, page 54; Stacey Jemison, page 173.
Illustrations: Dayanarra Pantig
https://thenounproject.com/icon/2466050/

Printed in China

25 24 23 22 21   1 2 3 4 5

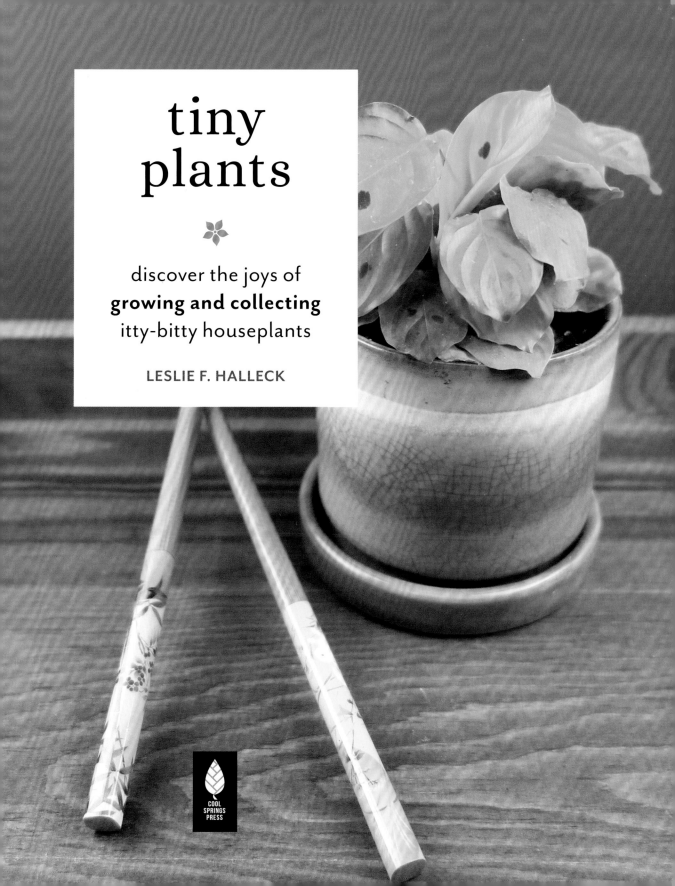

tiny plants

discover the joys of **growing and collecting** itty-bitty houseplants

LESLIE F. HALLECK

COOL SPRINGS PRESS

contents

preface

F I COULD TRACE my fascination with tiny plants back to a single moment, it would be my first in-person encounter with a Lilliputian orchid blooming in its native habitat. After college graduation, I headed for an internship in Puerto Rico with the Luquillo Long-Term Ecological Research (LTER) program. Embedded in the El Yunque National Rainforest, I assisted with research on the effects of Hurricane Hugo, which defoliated the entire rainforest in 1989. One day, while collecting data in a plot that included some large boulders, my eye caught the tiniest speck of pinkish red. As I approached, I realized with budding excitement that I had found a population of incredibly tiny orchids.

They were *Lepanthes rupestris*, lithophytic micro orchids only found in the Luquillo mountains of Puerto Rico. The flowers, only a few millimeters in size, rested directly on top of the tiny, 1-inch (2.5 cm) leaves. I recall jumping up and down—as I am prone to do when I discover cool plants and critters in their natural habitats. From that moment I was hooked on all things tiny. In addition to my formal research duties, I spent the next few months hunting down and studying all the tiny orchids and ferns I could find. In my subsequent travels—to the deep Amazon and Ecuadorian rainforests, as well as sky-high volcanoes—my eyes always sought out the tiniest botanical inhabitants.

Several years after that first encounter, I started building vivariums and keeping species of poison dart frogs and other herps. These small but intense living environments require specific plant species that are both small enough for the enclosure and appropriate for the animals. Once you start building vivariums for tiny animals, you inevitably take a deep dive into tiny plants.

As a professional horticulturist and lifelong plant collector and gardener, I have grown just about everything, in every type of setting—a dorm room, college apartment, or rental house; community garden plot; large, residential landscape; my closet; the garage; and in terrariums, in grow tents . . . you name it. Often, the "gateway drug" to the gardening hobby is an introduction to houseplants. I worked at a garden center through college, so my rental house was stuffed to the gills with every plant I could get my hands on. Luckily, my roommates, Kimberly and Jen, were tolerant of my plant obsession and did not complain *too* much about not being able to see out of the windows!

My varied gardening and plant obsessions have also waxed and waned over the years. I have spent some years fully immersed in my vegetable garden and beehives, while others were spent figuring out how to cram every species of blooming bulb or peach-colored English rose into my ornamental gardens. Yet, I always circle back to my love of houseplants, and collecting tiny specimens has brought me a lifetime of joy. I hope they can do the same for you.

→ I had to dig into an old box of printed film to find one photograph, albeit artistically blurry, of my original, in-person *Lepanthes rupestris* encounter.

introduction

Join me for a peek into the fascinating botanical world of perfectly petite plants. Learn how to collect and care for these tiny cuties as indoor windowsill plants or as plants grown under glass.

WHEN YOU COLLECT AND CARE for houseplants, you bring both serenity and style to your indoor life. Plant parents fill their social media feeds with millions of carefully curated and styled images of their most treasured plant specimens. What could be cuter—and more photogenic—than itty bitty houseplants?

Cuteness aside, tiny plants are the perfect choice for plant keepers with limited space and time. You may live in an apartment or small home and struggle to squeeze large leafy friends into crowded windowsills. If your home is dark, windowsill space with enough light might be limited. Perhaps you want to bring nature into a small office space or green up a corner of your desk. As your space overflows with the climbing *Monstera* and *Philodendron* you had no idea would get so big, tiny plants can feed your plant addiction without cramping your botanical style.

Imagine being able to keep *hundreds* of plant specimens even if you only have a small bit of spare space.

Beyond familiarity with a handful of small succulents, the breathtaking array of micro-houseplants is an unexplored world for most plant keepers. There are thousands upon thousands of tiny plant species to discover and collect. This book is an inspirational introduction to some of my favorite tiny plant species with big personalities.

In *Tiny Plants*, we'll dip our toes into the botany behind tiny plants and how they evolved, learn how to care for tiny houseplants, and explore a variety of tiny tropical foliage plants, micro orchids, itty-bitty succulents, and more for your windowsills and to grow under glass. From the most miniscule *Philodendron* species to the delicate blooms of the minute *Sinningia* to the teensiest carnivorous plants, you will no doubt discover many must-haves for your indoor plant collection. We will even have some fun with creative ways to style and display tiny plants.

Collecting and caring for tiny plants is a unique and rewarding hobby that is accessible to everyone, no matter the size of your space or level of experience. Whether you are just getting started with indoor plants or are a seasoned collector looking to rejuvenate your plant collection, *Tiny Plants* will inform and inspire.

→ A colony of Bladderwort, *Utricularia livida*, grows well in a teacup.

1

the botany of tiny plants

THERE IS SOMETHING MAGICAL and otherworldly about truly tiny plants. Often overlooked in natural habitats, tiny plant species, once discovered, reveal entirely new natural worlds and ecosystems. Botanical fascination aside, tiny plants are pretty darn cute, and that is what can make them so irresistible to plant collectors.

While there are many species of naturally tiny plants, not all plants found in the plant marketplace evolved on their own. Some are selected varieties (mutations) or cultivated hybrids, chosen from managed collections or cross-hybridized specifically for their genetically tiny potential. For some plants, the designation of "tiny" or "mini" may be relative to the standard size of parent or related species and varieties. I am an equal opportunity tiny plant lover, so we will touch on all these categories in this book.

Some tiny plants, on the other hand, have been forced to stay smaller than is natural, either by cultural practices, such as hard pruning, or by use of chemical growth inhibitors. Such plants typically revert to a normal, larger growth pattern once pruning halts, they are potted into a larger container, or they grow out of a chemical treatment. You will also find many photos online and on social media feeds of "tiny" plants that are simply in a seedling or juvenile phase and will grow much larger with time and maturity. While I am a big fan of artificial miniaturizing techniques, such as the art of Bonsai, I have steered clear of artificially tiny plants for our botanical journey.

Before we open the door to the world of tiny plant species you can grow—and how to grow them—let's first take a closer look at a bit of tiny plant botany. In nature, you'll find tiny plant species growing in many forms across all climates and geographical regions. In this book you'll find them categorized as terrestrial, epiphytic, lithophytic, or aquatic.

Evolution of Tiny Plants

Once mesmerized by a micro-orchid the size of your thumbnail—with a flower the size of a pinhead—you may wonder how on earth such a tiny plant exists. When so many other life-forms evolved to be as large as possible, what is the advantage of staying so tiny, and how have these plants survived?

Traditional thinking about plant evolution dictates that the bigger a plant is, the better it can compete for resources and dominate its environment. Following this logic, the bigger the plant species the better its chances for survival. Yet, emerging research shows that small plant species coexist with and *outnumber* large plant species in most environments.

As plants evolved over the millennia, leaf size—not just overall plant size—was key to successful evolution. Plants need their leaves to grow to the right size to harness enough light for photosynthesis without being so large that they lose too much water through transpiration.

Equatorial plants typically have larger leaves than those in drier climates, with the leaf size decreasing the farther you go from the equator. Plant scientists logically concluded that the

↑ Itty-bitty pygmy sundews, *Drosera lasiantha*, grow in wet, warm tropical and sub-tropical conditions.

← This miniature prayer plant, *Maranta repens*, growing in a 2½-inch (6 cm) pot, appears even smaller when placed beside a standard size *Calathea makoyana* growing in an 8-inch (20 cm) pot.

← Here is a close-up of a *Drosera patens* × *occidentalis* pygmy sundew in flower.

↑ I've mounted a few of my tiny tropical micro orchids on 2-inch (5 cm) sections of tree fern or wood with transparent fishing line. These micro-orchid species coexist with massive tropical plants in their native habitats.

↑ The traps on my tiny Australian pitcher plant hybrid, *Cephalotus follicularis* 'Agnes', are less than ½ inch (1.2 cm) in size.

increased water availability and humidity in equatorial tropical areas are key for plants to grow much bigger leaves; that the balance between absorbing sunlight and losing moisture were the sole factors in determining the size of plants and their leaves. In fact, we commonly associate wet tropical rainforests with big, large-leafed plants and dry regions, including deserts, with plants that have smaller leaves.

But if access to plentiful water and humidity inherently cause plants to evolve to be larger and have larger leaves, why do we find so many small to very tiny plants with small leaves in wet, tropical regions? And if bigger is always better, why do they outnumber the big plants?

Advantages of Being Tiny

There are a few possible explanations for the paradox of tiny plant evolution. Being small may simply afford a plant species more space and niche environments in which to grow and multiply. Lots of tiny plants can pack into tiny spaces. By producing tiny seeds, small plants also may have better "reproductive economy" than large plants. Smaller seeds (or other vegetative reproductive parts) are faster to produce and can make many more offspring, and generations, faster than large-seeded species. Size may enable tiny plants to exponentially outcompete in numbers, despite intense resource competition from large plants.

Leaf size is certainly related to access to soil and air moisture; where there is unlimited access to moisture, leaves adapted to such conditions can grow exceptionally large. However, since not all of them do, additional factors must be at play. What else might be encouraging plants to remain tiny in places where we would expect them to grow as large as possible? Additionally, why do we not find many large-leafed plants in wet, high-altitude environments? Air temperature—in terms of both degrees and fluctuation—seems to be the missing piece of the puzzle.

Leaf temperature relative to the surrounding air and fluctuations in those temperatures, especially freezing temperatures at night, may have much more to do with keeping leaf size small than ample access to water. Plants evolving in climates where cold or freezing temperatures are common at night have a better chance of survival if they have smaller leaves. The large surface area and thick leaf boundary layers (the area of still insulating air around the leaf surface) render large leaves less able to keep warm and more susceptible to cold damage.

→ This is most likely a specimen of *Peperomia rotundifolia* (or related species) I discovered while trekking through the Iquitos Amazon jungle region in Peru. Countless tiny plants grow tucked away amongst huge tropical trees, vines, and epiphytes.

↖ The small leaves of South African concrete leaf plant, *Titanopsis calcarea,* have a camouflage pattern that helps them blend into surrounding rocks. Plants grow in hot, rocky desert climates that can drop below freezing at night (plants tolerate down to 14°F [-10°C]).

↗ A local fly was nice enough to pose for scale with this "big" specimen of the tiny *Nototriche hartwegii* I encountered at about 18,000 ft (5,486 m) on the high páramo of the Chimborazo volcano, Ecuador. Daytime sunlight is intense and warm, but night temperatures plunge to -20°F (-28°C).

← Exceptionally large leaves, sported by many tropical aroids, can overheat in hot climates without enough humidity and root zone water. Conversely, they cannot efficiently absorb enough heat in climates with cold night temperatures.

Those same large leaves (with thick boundary layers) are also susceptible to overheating in hot, dry climates where there is not enough water availability at the root zone. Leaves cool off through water-loss via transpiration. The larger the leaf, the greater the surface area to cool, and the more water lost. If there is not enough root zone moisture to replenish that water, plants overheat and lose turgor pressure, and potentially die.

Essentially, plant survival in a given environment is a delicate balancing act between the amount of surface area over which a leaf will lose water through transpiration, the thickness of its boundary layer, water availability, and the air temperature around the leaf at night. Logically, as regions become warmer—or experience more dramatic fluctuations in temperature—and drier, plant evolution will trend towards smaller-leafed plant species to replace larger ones. The future is tiny.

Co-Evolution with Pollinators

When it comes to flowering plants, co-evolution with pollinators also plays a critical part in the success or failure of a species. Both plant and pollinator species depend on one another for survival and reproduction. If a tiny flowering plant species has a particularly successful pollination relationship with an equally successful pollinator, it can reproduce more quickly and in bigger numbers.

Orchids typically have monogamous relationships with their pollinator species. Orchid flowers often mimic the shape and colors of either the female or the male pollinator, tricking the pollinator into trying to mate with it, and thereby spreading around pollen from flower to flower. We call this botanical fake-out "sexual deception." Micro orchid species often pair up with such pollinator partners as tiny bees, wasps, flies, and even fungus gnats. Relations between orchids and their pollinators have been so successful, in fact, that orchids make up about 10 percent of all flowering plant species on Earth.

The co-dependent dynamic with tiny insect pollinators influences tiny flowering plant species to stay tiny, regardless of water availability—as long as their pollinator populations remain healthy.

As a plant collector, be aware that almost 40% of all terrestrial plant species are already categorized as very rare and at risk for extinction. Recently published research also suggests that 40% of all insect species are in decline and could become extinct over the next decade. With the insects go the plants, and vice versa. Habitat destruction and over-collection are both serious threats. When you purchase novelty plant species, do your research into the vendor, and make sure they are propagating their plants in "captivity," not selling plants collected from the wild. Always make sure foreign and overseas online plant vendors include a phytosanitary certificate with your order to ensure legitimacy and legality.

FUN FACT One of the smallest bees in the world, *Perdita minima*, grows to less than 9/100 inch (2 mm) long and pollinates the tiny flowers of many small-growing *Euphorbia* (spurge) species.

→ This tiny insect is pollinating a miniature orchid.

Where Tiny Plants Grow

In nature, tiny plant species grow in many forms across all climates and geographical regions, and in many different micro habitats. This book provides the growing designations for terrestrial, epiphyte, hemiepiphyte, lithophyte, and aquatic. While these categories can get much more complicated and are further divided in the academic world of botany, I stuck to basic definitions for our purposes.

Terrestrial Terrestrial plants are land-growing plants with a primary root system that anchors into or on top of soil or rocks. These roots take up water and nutrients from the soil or surrounding organic matter.

↑ This lovely colony of *Bulbophyllum* sp.—an epiphytic orchid— grows on tree bark in the Longwood Gardens Orchid Conservatory.

Epiphyte Epiphytes germinate and grow on other plants (non-parasitically) by attaching themselves to nearby trees and vegetation. Good examples are many orchids, bromeliads, and tillandsia. Tiny epiphytic plants are some of the most fascinating to collect. I am especially obsessed with tiny micro orchids, many of which fall into this category. You can grow epiphytic species mounted on pieces of driftwood, tree fern fiber, mosses, and the like. They often grow well in a loose, chopped moss mixture or orchid bark mix planted in porous pots.

↑ Tropical plants, such as *Philodendron* and *Scindapsus*, will grow in pots or as epiphytic vines.

Hemiepiphyte Also referred to as semi-epiphytes, hemiepiphytes may germinate either on other plants or on the ground, and either send down roots to grow in the soil or send up vines with aerial roots that attach to surrounding plants. Some hemiepiphytes may spend one stage of development growing terrestrially or epiphytically, then transition to the opposite as they mature. They may also completely lose their terrestrial form once vines become epiphytic. Good examples are species in the genera of *Monstera*, *Philodendron*, and *Syngonium*.

Think of your *Monstera* plant growing in a pot that is sending up vines with aerial roots on a moss pole. Most of the tiny ferns featured in this book are also hemiepiphytes and are versatile houseplants that can be grown in several different ways.

↑ Liverwort, a lithophyte, grows on rocks.

↑ I discovered this tiny begonia growing between cracks in the rocks atop Huayna Picchu, Peru.

Lithophyte Lithophytes are an interesting group of plants that grow in or around rocks. They are also referred to as epipetric or epilithic plants. They absorb nutrients from rainwater and surrounding decomposing plant litter. Lithophytes that can only grow on rocks are called obligate lithophytes. Those that can grow both on rocks and on soil are called facultative lithophytes. Examples of lithophytes include algae, liverworts, butterworts, many ferns, and some species of orchids, such as *Lepanthes* and *Paphiopedilum.*

Chasmophyte Chasmophytes grow in the crevasses and fissures in rocks where organic matter and soil have accumulated. Many carnivorous plants and certain begonias and primrose fall into this category.

Liverworts, hornworts, and mosses are non-vascular plants informally grouped together and referred to as bryophytes. Many bryophytes grow alongside other lithophytes and chasmophytes, and they are an important part of these unique tiny plant communities.

Aquatic Aquatic plants grow either totally submersed (below the water) as true aquatics or emersed (foliage just above the water) in fresh or salt water. Some must always be submersed, while the needs of others vary by season. Some, such as *Anubias* and *Hydrocotyle* featured in this book, are even adaptable enough to classify as both aquatic *and* terrestrial. They often grow best when emersed or mounted ephiphytically in a humid aquarium, rather than submersed. These types of plants are also classified as semiaquatic.

You can grow and collect tiny plant species indoors in many ways and keep them in a variety of containers and enclosed growing environments. Creating the most favorable artificial conditions for tiny plants involves getting to know more about the individual species and where and how it grows in its natural environment. I encourage you to take a deeper botanical dive into each plant species you bring into your tiny plant collection.

↓ Emersed aquatic plants, such lotus and waterlilies, grow with their roots either floating under water or clinging into banks or the soil. Their leaves grow above the water or float on top.

2

collecting and caring for tiny plants

COLLECTING AND GROWING tiny plants is an intimate affair. You may discover the way you interact with and care for your tiniest plants feels a bit more personal than it does with larger houseplants. While I tend to have a survival-of-the-fittest approach with my big houseplants—unless, of course, it happens to be a rare or expensive specimen—I tend to dote daily over my tiny plant companions. They are just more precious to me.

Tiny plants do require some different care strategies than larger houseplants. Even so, given the small space they occupy, it is relatively simple to accommodate their unique needs. Some tiny plants will be easier to care for than larger tropicals.

Care Practices

Knowing how a species of plant grows in its natural habitat is crucial to growing it successfully indoors. In some ways tiny plants can be easier to care for and do not take up much space. You certainly will not need the same volume of potting mix, water, fertilizer, or other supplies to maintain tiny plants. They can also involve less mess than larger indoor plants. That said, some tiny plants may need more attention when it comes to their watering needs and they can be more sensitive to temperature and humidity.

For each species of plant highlighted in the book, I provide basic care parameters and techniques to guide you. Some conditions will be a firm requirement; however, what works for you may differ from my recommendations based on your growing conditions and habits. Growing your green thumb and learning to intuit what plants need comes with time, patience, and a lot of hands-on experience. You and your tiny plants must develop your own personal relationship, within your home and its unique environment.

Get to know your space, the natural light volume, temperature, and relative humidity, and test out plants in different locations to find the right combination. Experimentation is the key to success.

↑ One of my *Haworthia angustifolia* specimens growing in a tiny 1½-inch (4 cm) terracotta pot is about to bloom!

↑ *Peperomia prostrata* is small enough to grow in one of my tiny 1½ inch (4 cm) handmade glazed ceramic pots.

Do not stress or feel guilty if you do not get it "right" with a plant species the first time around—or the second or third time! I always tell new plant parents that losing a plant teaches you how to grow it better the next time. Plus, if you learn some basic plant propagation skills, you can always make *more* plants. Remember, green thumbs are grown, not born!

Contain Your Tiny Plants

One of my favorite aspects of growing tiny plants is the variety of vessels—tiny teacups, thimbles, seashells, herb jars—that you can repurpose as growing containers for them. Many of the tiny ceramic glazed pots featured in this book were handmade for me by a local potter. I love the uniqueness of handmade pottery, and these days you can find many more handmade planters for very tiny plant specimens.

Most tiny plants need tiny pots. But each species will have its own space and moisture requirement and a type of container for which they are best suited. Some of the tiniest sundews need a larger container than most of the other plants in this book. Why? Because as tiny as a pygmy sundew is, its relatively long tap roots and preference for "wet feet" means it needs a tall container that holds a relatively large soil volume.

Conversely, you can grow many succulents, such as living stones, in tiny pots barely bigger than the plants themselves. A succulent or cactus, which need to dry more between waterings, can thrive in a relatively small container with less soil. Some moisture-loving plants, such as micro-Sinningia, have such a tiny root system they need only a pot the size of a thimble to thrive. It all comes down to the plant's root morphology and how much root zone moisture it requires.

When you pot a plant in a tiny planter, leave about ⅛ inch (0.3 cm) from the lip of the pot to the soil level, so that water does not spill out over the edge.

↑ Unsealed clay pots with drainage holes (these range in size from 1 to 3 inches [2.5 to 8 cm] wide) are conducive to air movement.

↑ To reduce water loss from porous clay pots, use a pot sealer followed by a primer and paint of your choice.

TYPES OF CONTAINERS
Materials

The material from which your container is made is an important consideration. Unglazed clay or unsealed concrete pots allow water and air to move through the porous material. The air movement is beneficial for plants that do not like wet feet; but it also means soil in porous pots will dry faster. I like to use unglazed porous containers for succulent and cactus species or other plants that benefit from drying between waterings and for tropical species or epiphytes that need good root aeration under glass.

Sealed glazed pottery, or plastic and glass, will hold more moisture and limit air circulation at the root zone. Sealed materials are beneficial for plants, such as most tropical terrestrial plants or semi-aquatic species, that suffer when they dry out. If you grow a tropical species in a porous clay pot and it regularly dries out too fast, repot it into non-porous sealed pottery, plastic, or glass to retain more moisture.

Drainage

Containers with drainage holes are necessary for most tiny terrestrial and epiphytic plants, even moisture-loving ones. Plants can quickly rot in containers with no drainage due to a lack of oxygen at the root zone, which leads to disease and decay. You can get away with using containers with no drainage when growing some high-humidity epiphytic or semi-epiphytic species, such as some of the micro orchids, epiphytic vines, rhizomatous ferns, or certain gesneriads. For such plants in a drainless container, use a mixture of chopped moss, orchid bark, and a small amount of potting mix, instead of a potting soil. Certain carnivorous plants, such as butterworts and bladderworts, will also grow successfully in watertight vessels in an appropriate growing media.

In general, if repurposing small vessels, such as teacups, as planting containers, it is best to add a drainage hole if possible.

TERRARIUMS

Once you start collecting tiny plants, you will discover all sorts of enclosures you can use to keep mixed collections or individual specimens. Terrariums are a common container for tiny plants. *Full disclosure*: This is not a terrarium building or care book. There are many other comprehensive books available on how to build, plant, and maintain planted, watertight or sealed terrariums. Closed planted terrariums and vivariums are special micro-environments with many different requirements and environmental controls—and growing challenges—that we will not dive deep into here. We will, however, cover basic definitions of several types of enclosed growing systems and some basic tips on how to properly layer a planted terrarium.

WARDIAN CASE: The Wardian case, an early form of what we now call a terrarium, contains and protects potted plant specimens. Botanist Dr. Nathaniel Bagshaw Ward (and another botanist, A.A. Maconochie, a bit earlier) invented it to successfully ship precious plant specimens back to Europe from around the world. Prized plant specimens that were collected often died on their shipping journey. Sealed glass glazed Wardian cases protected and sustained potted plant specimens in transit, allowing access to light and recycled freshwater trapped inside the case. In fact, Wardian cases are to thank for much of our modern access to fruit and flowers, including important crops, such as coffee and sugar.

Wardian cases typically have a solid base or reservoir in which you set potted plants. Use water trays or liners to catch water from the pots. The plants are then covered or enclosed by a wood- or metal-framed glass cover. There may be a door that can be opened and closed, or the solid glass cover sits on top of the base. Use Wardian cases to keep collections of potted plants that may require a bit more humidity or warmth than your home windowsill provides. Wardian cases provide the flexibility to move high-humidity potted plants in and out of the case to temporarily display in other locations or trade out plants seasonally. You can camouflage pots with mosses to make them look more like planted terrariums.

Many modern-day interpretations of Wardian cases are not truly soil- or watertight, even though many are sold as plantable terrariums. While a fancy one can up your plant style, you can also use simple glass jars and canisters with lids; vintage clear glass canisters with interesting shapes are fun finds. These make mini Wardian cases that allow much more flexibility with your tiny, high-humidity specimens. You can easily move them around, placing them under grow lighting or for display.

→ Tiny fern, *Lemmaphyllum microphyllum*, is content growing in a 2-inch (5 cm) pot inside a glass jar.

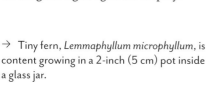

TOP LEFT: My potted *Pleurothallis costaricensis* orchid resides in a tiny modern version of a Wardian case with a hinged door. The case helps increase humidity around the plant without making it too wet. TOP RIGHT: *Pleurothallis costaricensis* orchid is in bloom thanks to the extra humidity. BOTTOM: One of my nicer handmade Wardian cases with potted *Sinningia* and *Saintpaulia* in bloom and on display under glass.

CLOSED PLANTED TERRARIUM: Though you can control its humidity via an adjustable door or lid, a properly assembled closed terrarium is its own micro-ecosystem with its water, air, and substrate separated from the surrounding environment. Use any glass or acrylic vessel that is watertight to create a closed planted terrarium; watertight aquariums work well. You can leave a successful terrarium of this type sealed for many years, or may choose to interact with, regularly maintain, or modify it now and then.

If you *do* want to plant directly into a closed terrarium, you must create some artificial drainage to direct water away from the plant's root zone. This involves creating specific layers of different substrates, such as gravel, charcoal, and planting mix. Insert a thin biologic draining mesh filter cut to size between each layer to keep them from mixing.

TERRARIUM LAYERS:

1. False bottom: Layer gravel, rocks, or crushed glass at least 1 inch (2.5 cm) deep in the base of the terrarium. Place a cut mesh layer on top.

2. Filtration: Include a ½-inch (1.3 cm) layer of activated charcoal or biochar. Place a cut mesh layer on top.

3. Moisture wicking: Add a ½- to 1-inch (1.3 to 2.5 cm) layer of sphagnum moss, then layer mesh (optional).

4. Soil: Use a terrarium potting mix adjusted for plant species.

5. Add direct-planted specimens.

6. Cover any open soil surface with mosses, decorative stone or glass, etc.

Depending on what you plant into a closed terrarium, you may need to provide some artificial air circulation (fans) or venting, artificial light, and possibly temperature control. Closed terrariums do not have to be directly planted; they are also perfect for housing collections of potted high-humidity plants, as with a Wardian case.

> Depth of each layer is relative to the size and height of the terrarium. Some terrarium builders put the activated charcoal layer underneath the gravel layer. Vivariums with live animals may require additional layers of moss and leaf litter, so do your homework!

→ A closed planted terrarium needs drainage layers to keep plants healthy.

OPPOSITE PAGE: My miniature *Dendrobium cuthbertsonii* 'Pink Giant' HCC/AOS × bicolor, 'Orange', planted on moss, grows under glass in a cool-temperature room.

OPEN TERRARIUM: There are many variations of open-top watertight (or semi-watertight) glass vessels or bowls sold as terrariums; also referred to as bowl terrariums, bubble bowls, or bowl planters. You will often see open glass vessels commonly directly planted with succulents or other low-humidity plants. I do not consider these vessels true terrariums, rather simply glass planters or vases.

Plants such as begonias, African violets, other gesneriads, some tropical foliage and ferns, and certain carnivorous plants, such as butterworts and bladderworts, do very well planted directly into open terrariums and bubble bowls. But remember, there is no drainage, so follow the same layering guidelines as for closed terrariums.

Open terrariums can provide a little extra humidity for certain plants if you add a moisture-holding substrate, gravel, or moistened moss. You can also set potted plants into open terrariums, then camouflage the pots with gravel or mosses, which will help to slightly increase humidity. I often keep groups of larger potted *Sinningia* hybrids, African violets, or mini orchids that appreciate extra humidity, but can tolerate drying between waterings, in open terrariums.

I generally do not recommend directly planting succulents or cacti into open terrariums with no drainage; it is simply too easy to overwater them and suffocate their root system. If there is sufficiently high light volume for long enough each day and limited water, you can pull it off with less challenging succulent or cactus species, such as *Haworthia*. Unfortunately, many beginners who try terrarium planting with succulents or cacti indoors place plants in low-light conditions, resulting in overwatering and plant death. It is better to set potted succulents into open terrariums and hide the pots.

↑ Succulents and cacti planted directly into drainless bowls or closed terrariums often rot.

→ A miniature orchid set inside an open hanging "terrarium" tolerates a bit of drying between waterings.

↑ This open-top terrarium provides just enough extra humidity for plants to thrive.

ORCHIDARIUM: This modern take on the Wardian case is typically used to keep micro- and miniature-orchids in pots or mounted on bark, but you can include other high-humidity species. Orchidariums offer a more advanced method for keeping and growing species that need good air circulation but are also sensitive to humidity and temperature levels. Circulation fans, automated misting, grow lights, and temperature controls are integrated to address these factors with precision. Build your own orchidarium using an aquarium, vivarium case, or grow tent; or, seek out plug-and-play options.

↑ This commercially available plug-and-play orchidarium comes complete with automated air circulation, humidity fogger, and grow lighting.

VIVARIUM: The Latin word vivarium translates to a "place of life," and the term is most often used to describe an enclosure that is suitable for sustaining animal life in conjunction with plant life. In a vivarium, you must consider how the substrate will break down and filter toxins and waste from the animals and how you will control temperature and humidity. Vivariums are enclosed with small doors you can open for venting or cleaning. How you build a vivarium and which species of plants you can include depends on the animal species you intend to house. For many years I built vivariums for various species of poison dart frogs, which benefit from certain types and sizes of plants on which to perch and feed and that provide protection for reproduction. Many of the tiny, high-humidity ferns, aroids, and micro orchids featured in this book are excellent additions to vivariums.

PALUDARIUM: One quarter to one half of these enclosures is water, housing fish or other aquatic animals, as well as aquatic plants. The remainder contains direct-planted or mounted plants and may also accommodate terrestrial animals. Most are enclosed, with a lid that can be opened and closed, and typically require artificial grow lighting. Many vivariums for keeping poison dart frogs are paludariums.

RIPARIUM: A riparium enclosure mimics a shoreline ecosystem. Half filled with water, the tank or other vessel also contains aquatic plants, as well as hardscape terrain to support semi-aquatic, moisture-loving tropical plants. Most ripariums are open or widely vented at the top. Small ripariums are excellent choices for the small aquatic and semi-aquatic species featured in this book.

AQUARIUM: Aquariums are fully aquatic enclosures that support aquatic animals and/or aquatic plants. Whether it is completely enclosed or vented depends on the oxygenation needs of what it contains.

If you grow groups of plants in the same terrarium or case, make sure any combination of species you choose has similar environmental and care requirements. You're not obliged to grow more than one species together, however. I grow most of my tiny plant species as individual specimens, each with its own container.

↓ This paludarium houses aquatic and terrestrial animals, as wells as many types of plants.

Be aware that bright light and high humidity often encourage algae to grow in closed terrariums, Wardian cases, and on plants in glass vessels. If a lot of water is condensing on the inside of the glass for most of the day, it is time to vent the terrarium or glass case. Wipe down the inside of the glass to remove excess moisture and algae.

Growing Media

Ideal growing media or substrate varies for each type of plant, based on its native habitat. Growing media matters more than you might think and is often at the root of struggles new plant parents experience.

POTTING MIX: Tropical plants grown indoors generally do well in a soilless (sterile), lightweight potting mix with good drainage. I often mix in coir (coco fiber) as a peat substitute both to lighten mixes and help maintain consistent moisture without sogginess. Starting with a soilless potting mix helps reduce fungal and bacterial problems. Combinations of peat, coir, chopped sphagnum moss, vermiculite, and horticultural perlite are common, and you can easily blend them together to create your own mix.

POTTING SOIL: Potting soils contain some amount of organic matter, usually in the form of compost, worm castings, or other composted manures. Small amounts of organic matter—say 10 percent to no more than 20 percent—can be good for some indoor plants. However, heavy organic potting soils with more organic matter are best left for outdoor potted plants in larger containers. Indoors, potting soils with organic matter can breed pests, such as fungus gnats and fungal or bacterial growth. They also hold too much water for potted plants, especially those grown under glass. Experiment with what works best for you and the types of plants you grow.

COIR: A lightweight fiber material made from coconut husks as a byproduct of coconut production, coir is not only excellent at holding moisture and aerating soil, it is a renewable resource.

PEAT MOSS: This decomposed organic matter mined from peat bogs improves water retention. Peat moss is a non-renewable resource, as it takes centuries to develop and harvesting it removes the living layer of the bog above it.

PERLITE: Made from volcanic glass heated to form small white balls, perlite aerates the mix and improves drainage.

VERMICULITE: This material, made from hydrated magnesium dialuminium iron silicate, lightens seed-starting and specialty potting mixes.

CHOPPED SPHAGNUM MOSS: Sphagnum moss is a live moss that holds moisture and is used to grow many epiphytes and root cuttings. Finely chopped it can also be added to potting mixes to lighten and retain moisture.

CHARCOAL OR BIOCHAR: Horticultural charcoal can help plants and planted terrarium environments by increasing water absorption, influencing pH, binding toxins, and encouraging beneficial microbes.

↑ My ox tongue plant (*Gasteria glomerata*) grows happily in a 3-inch (8 cm) pot with a 50/50 mixture of succulent potting soil and decomposed granite.

↑ I planted my tiny pitcher plant, *Cephalotus follicularis* 'Agnes', in a 3-inch (8 cm) pot in a heavy sandy mix that stays moist all the time and can also support moss growth.

LECA: Lightweight expanded clay aggregate (Leca) absorbs water and air, expanding slightly when soaked. These small, inert baked clay balls provide a porous surface onto which roots can latch and are used to grow plants hydroponically or aquaponically.

TREE BARK AND DRIFTWOOD: You can mount epiphytes directly on tree bark and driftwood, usually with a small padding of sphagnum moss.

TREE FERN FIBER: The dried fiber from inside tree fern trunks makes the perfect backing (wall) for terrariums and vivariums. Mount epiphytes to it or allow semi-epiphytic vines to grow and root into the fiber.

HYGROLON: This inert synthetic fiber created to mimic porous tree bark and wick water is useful for mounting epiphytes, tropical vines, and mosses. Some manufacturers fit their Hygrolon products with inner wires that allow you to shape "branches" in different directions. Although created to reduce harvest of the natural products it mimics, Hygrolon is non-biodegradable.

← Tree bark and Hygrolon function similarly but the latter is a synthetic product.

↑ Orchid bark, horticultural charcoal, and chopped sphagnum moss are all useful in growing tiny plants. See the small white perlite mixed with the orchid bark.

↑ Baby *Bolbitis* fern is small enough for a teacup filled with water and Leca.

GROWING MEDIA BY PLANT TYPE

EPIPHYTIC AND HEMIEPIPHYTIC PLANTS need high humidity, but they also need good air circulation around their roots. Pot epiphytic or hemiepiphytic species into containers using a chunky orchid bark mix or chopped moss as a potting mix.

MOST GESNERIADS, such as African violets, gloxinias, sinningia, and begonias, need substrates that both hold moisture and drain well. Look for potting mixes labeled for African violets to grow these plants. If you want to mix your own, follow this version of a potting mix recipe for such species developed by Michael Kartuz of Kartuz Greenhouses. To throw down some old school horticultural lingo, refer to this recipe as G-B-S mix (Gesneriad-Begonia-Saintpaulia).

G-B-S Mix

4 parts sphagnum peat moss
   (I prefer to substitute Coir)
4 parts perlite

1 part vermiculite (optional)
A sprinkle of ground limestone (1 tablespoon [40 g] to 9 total quarts [2.5 kg] of mixture)

Combine ingredients in ratio to each other. Mix with some warm rainwater or purified water to moisten before use.

SUCCULENTS AND CACTI need good root support but also need lots of air pockets and good drainage of water away from the roots. Succulent and cactus mix may contain mixtures of grit, sand, perlite, or coir fiber to create a well-aerated mix that drains quickly.

CARNIVOROUS PLANTS have a wide variety of growing media needs. Many species grow in peat-heavy moist soils, some in more sandy soils, while still others grow in straight sphagnum moss or in rocky substrates. Do your research on each species to make sure to buy or mix the appropriate substrate.

Manage Water and Humidity

Managing water and humidity for tiny plants can be easier *or* more challenging… it just depends on the plant species and your personal plant care habits. The smaller the container and soil volume, the quicker plants will dry between waterings. Tiny tropical plants kept in tiny pots out in the open, versus a terrarium or glass container, will need more frequent watering. If you are by nature a heavy-handed waterer, growing plants in smaller containers can help you minimize overwatering—especially with succulents and cacti. If you are struggling with over-watering any of your houseplants, repotting them into a slightly smaller container can help better manage soil moisture at the root zone.

That said, be warned there are some tiny plant species that will turn to mush simply at the sight of a watering can (I'm talking to *you, Lithops lesliei*), even when they're grown in the tiniest of containers. You will need to get to know your tiny plant species' water preferences.

WATER QUALITY

First, let's review the different types of water, treated and untreated, you will use to water tiny plants. It is often recommended that certain types of plant only be watered with rainwater or distilled or purified water. If a plant comes with this recommendation, it is for good reason and you should adhere.

Rainwater I prefer to water most of my houseplants with rainwater I collect in rain barrels placed around my roofline gutters. Collecting rainwater can also be as simple as setting out buckets on a balcony or patio. While I might resort to tap water now and then for some of my larger, hardier houseplants, I *never* water my micro orchids or carnivorous plants with any-thing but rainwater. Rainwater is a purer source of water, without all the toxic salts, minerals, and chemical treatments found in tap water. It can also contain beneficial organic matter and minerals for your plants.

That is not to say rainwater does not contain some contaminates or non-beneficial organic matter. There may be components leaching from my roof, algae, or animal excrement that make it into my collected water. It might even contain mosquito or other insect larvae, so make sure to put a porous cover over the collection bucket. Still, it is usually the healthiest option for your plants, especially the sensitive ones. Is it a bit more of a hassle to collect and use rainwa-ter on my plants? Of course. But there is no point in buying a pricey micro-orchid or specialty carnivorous plant just to kill it with tap water.

Tap water Tap water varies widely by municipality. Generally, there are salts (inorganic min-erals) and chemicals in tap water that can build up and be toxic to houseplants. Water that is softened contains a lot of sodium, which is especially damaging to houseplants, as it inhibits water uptake. Many common houseplants will tolerate unsoftened tap water, for a time. But if there is fluoride in your tap water, it can also build up and stress many species. Some tap water is treated to have a higher pH to prevent corrosion of pipes. Plants that prefer more acidic conditions, such as African violets or orchids, will not be too happy if their water has a high

← I fill recycled wine bottles with rainwater and store them around my home for easy watering, or to fill squirt and spray bottles.

pH. Well water is often extremely hard due to the minerals in surrounding bedrock. It may also contain a lot of sulfur, which can also be toxic to plants.

If you regularly water with tap water, you may see a white film develop on top of the soil. This is usually salt build up (if it is not fungus). Salt build up is more common in soils that are heavier and do not drain as quickly. It's best to repot the plant with fresh potting soil more often if you use tap water. You can also leach the soil (drench it) with purified water every two to three months to remove excess salts.

Distilled water The collected steam or condensation of boiled or vaporized water, distilled water is a type of purified water that is a good choice for houseplants. The process leaves behind contaminants and minerals, which do not vaporize, but does not always remove all chemicals, such as chloramines. DIY distillation is a hassle, but you can purchase small kits for at-home use or simply purchase bottled distilled water. Boiling rainwater or tap water will also potentially kill any harmful bacteria or other non-beneficial organisms.

Dechlorinated water Chlorine, which is toxic to plants, may be added to municipal tap water for sanitation. To naturally dechlorinate tap water, simply set it in an open container that is exposed to light for twenty-four hours. Chlorine will naturally break down over this period. This is something simple you can do to slightly improve tap water for houseplants. However, if your city uses chloramine instead of chlorine, this method does not work. Check with your city water department to confirm water additives.

Reverse osmosis Reverse osmosis (RO) is a purification process that uses a filtration step to remove all inorganic minerals and contaminants, such salts, heavy metals, chloramine, and organic matter. Water filtered through reverse osmosis is the "cleanest" water for plants and drinking water. If you have a RO filtration system in your home, this water is safe to use on plants.

Both distilled and reverse osmosis filtered water are considered purified water, but RO water is technically cleaner, void of all potential inorganic and organic minerals and contaminants. Know that without inorganic minerals and organic matter in the water, you will need to provide all the additional nutrients plants need through supplemental fertilization.

WATERING METHODS

Bottom watering Often, when you try to water your plant, water will run off the top of the soil or moss, rather than saturate the soil or root system. Because tiny pots will dry out more quickly, it is important to make sure to wet the entire root system.

Bottom watering is an easy way to thoroughly saturate the soil in tiny pots, without getting water onto the plant foliage. Bottom watering is especially handy for hydrating plants with deep feeder roots, such as sundews; or plants sensitive to water on their foliage, such as African violets. Simply set the pot (with a drainage hole) into a shallow water tray with ½ to 1 inch (1.3 to 2.5 cm) of water and allow the soil in the pot to draw up the water. When the surface of the potting mix is moist, you can remove the plant from the water. Do not let the plant sit in the water indefinitely. That said, some carnivorous or aquatic species will need to sit in 1 to 2 inches (2.5 to 5 cm) of standing bottom water at all times.

If you use purified water, it will typically have a neutral pH of about 7.0. Depending on the species of plant (terrestrial or aquatic), you may want to use fertilizers that slightly acidify the water, or growing medium, if using water with a pH of 7 or higher.

→ My tiny pygmy sundews soak up bottom water from a tray.

Wick watering Many plants benefit from a wick watering system. For plants that need consistent moisture but cannot sit in soggy or boggy conditions—or do not tolerate water on their leaves—wick watering is a good solution.

Use just about any vessel that holds water and can also support the plant pot above the water line. Using some wicking twine (synthetic materials won't break down in the water), press one end into the potting soil of the container through the drainage hole (or thread the wick through the bottom of the pot when you repot the plant), then submerge the bottom of the wick into the water. The wick will draw up a constant source of water from the reservoir to the root zone.

You can also find many two-part self-watering containers that come with a pot for planting along with a water reservoir; these types of pots may also be called Oyama pots. Some self-watering planters use porous clay to absorb water from the reservoir, while others use a wicking system. African violets and many other gesneriads do very well with wick-watering or Oyama pots.

← A hole cut in the top of this simple plastic storage container makes a perfect potholder and water reservoir for a wick-watering system for this micromini African violet.

Swamp watering When managing water for plants with root zones that should never dry out completely but also need air circulation around their epiphytic roots, you can use what I refer to as swamp watering. It's sort of a variation on bottom watering. Set a mounted orchid (or other mounted epiphyte) in a shallow, watertight container or dish filled with a small amount of water—just enough to contact the root zone or mounting materials that will absorb or wick it. You may also add some moistened sphagnum moss that you keep wet all the time. This is an especially handy technique for micro orchids that are mounted on small pieces of bark or sticks, or on pieces of tree fern fiber, but need constant access to moisture at their root zone. For micro orchids, such as *Haraella retrocalla*, that prefer good air circulation but still need regular moisture at their root zone, I fill teacups with some rainwater and sphagnum moss and set the mounted plant in the cup.

↑ My Taiwan fragrant orchid (*Haraella retrocalla*) likes a consistently moist (not wet) root zone, and benefits from swamp method watering.

↑ Note the level of water in this teacup, where the roots of my *Sedirea japonica* miniature orchid rests touching the water to absorb it into the mounted sphagnum moss.

← This lovely shot glass makes the perfect wick-watering reservoir for one of my little sinningia growing in a 1½-inch (4 cm) pot.

Squirt bottle Watering tiny plants in tiny pots, especially succulents, can be a tricky to accomplish with a regular size watering can, or even a small water cup. Water quickly overflows from the top of the pot washing growing media away with it. You may not even be able to fit the watering tip under the plants' tiny foliage. Small squeeze bottles with pointed tips are perfect for watering tiny potted plants and epiphytes mounted on bark or in baskets. Squirt bottle watering is especially handy to keep water off the foliage of succulents, cacti, and gesneriads.

HUMIDITY

Many tropical plants require a medium to high relative humidity to survive and thrive. Humidity is always relative to temperature. Simply stated, relative humidity equals the amount of water vapor in the air compared to how much the air *can* hold at a specific temperature. If relative humidity at 75°F (24°C) is 50 percent, the air is holding 50 percent of the water vapor it can hold at that temperature. This is an ideal range for most tropical windowsill plants. If the temperature gets warmer and the amount of water vapor in the air stays the same, then the relative humidity decreases. If the temperature gets colder, then the relative humidity increases.

Humidity impacts plant turgor pressure (the amount of water in plant cells). Through the process of transpiration, plants exchange water and gasses through the small pores (stomata) in their leaves. The higher the relative air humidity, the slower plants will lose water through transpiration. When relative humidity is low, water may be pulled up and out of the plants more quickly, causing them to wilt (or die). For many plants, such as African violets, the warmer the temperature the higher the relative humidity they will need. However, if temperatures are hot and relative humidity is also high, some plants can overheat because they cannot transpire quickly enough. Low temperatures and high humidity, on the other hand, is a common cause of mildew growth. Matching the plant species to right balance of environmental conditions is always the trick.

← Left out in the open for only two days, this miniature oakleaf fig shriveled right up! I keep this tiny tropical vine under glass in high relative humidity.

→ Plastic squirt bottles are often the best way to water tiny plants—both potted and mounted.

Understanding target humidity ranges for different plants can be a little confusing for beginners—*and* experienced growers! For example, African violets grow in relative humidity ranges from 70 to 80 percent in their natural habitat. But in a standard home—in artificial windowsill culture—they fair well with 50 to 60 percent relative humidity. You'll need to experiment with different plant species to learn how they respond to your home's environmental conditions.

If you have extra time on your hands or work from home and can mist plants two or three times per day, then you can get away with growing certain high-humidity terrestrial and epiphytic plants out in the open. It will just take some time and practice to get to know your plants and how they will respond to the given environment and humidity levels.

Humidifiers and foggers

In an open room, you may consider using a humidifier if tropical plants are struggling. Humidifiers may have a built-in water reservoir or have a water pump. They generally produce larger water droplets. Some new small humidifiers on the market are useful for setting near small groups of houseplants. While humidifiers can help to *slightly* increase relative humidity in the open, they work best in small spaces. That said, undesirable mildew growth in fabrics, carpets, or wood can result. Know that if you are running air conditioning to cool your home, the AC system will continually work to remove this moisture from the air to cool air temperature. Humidifiers work very well in grow tents or in larger shelving systems covered with a plastic tent.

Cool foggers, or atomizers, do essentially the same thing as larger humidifiers. The difference is they are much smaller and do not have a water reservoir or water pump. Submerge the fogger into a water tray, and it turns that water into cool fog (very tiny water droplets). Use foggers to increase the relative humidity in an enclosed Wardian case, paludarium, terrarium, or vivarium. I use a fogger inside my orchidarium, with a reservoir of rainwater, to keep relative humidity between 75 and 90 percent for my humidity-sensitive micro orchids and other species. A small recirculating fan keeps the air and fog moving. *Note that some foggers will not function properly with distilled or purified water and will only work with rainwater or tap water.*

← A fogger produces cool mist in my orchidarium.

Misting

To mist or not to mist? Not all plant parents agree on whether misting is beneficial, but in my experience it all comes down to the individual plant species and your home's environment. While misting the air around plants daily is not going to have much impact on the surrounding humidity, a fine mist of water onto the foliage of some species can help slow water loss to transpiration.

That said, misting water *on* the plant leaves without good air movement—especially with large water droplets—can encourage certain fungal and bacterial diseases. If you must mist, spray a fine mist of water above or on plants in the morning so that foliage does not sit wet overnight in the dark, which can encourage disease.

If misting a larger volume of water directly onto foliage and stems, what you are really doing is *watering*, not misting. Heavy, direct misting is a good way to water many epiphytes, hemiepiphytes, and vining plants with aerial roots.

If you are growing high-humidity plants in an open terrarium or bubble bowl, you may need to mist above plants daily.

It is best practice to avoid misting water directly onto plants with fuzzy leaves, such as African violets and many succulents. Begonias and many gesneriads also do not appreciate water sitting on their leaves, which can result in damage or decay. However, some fuzzy ferns won't at all mind water on their foliage.

← Use misters or small spray bottles to mist both windowsill plants and those in open or closed terrariums.

↑ My tiny *Syngonium* 'Pink Petite 'sits in a gravel humidity tray.

Humidity tray

Humidity or pebble trays are often recommended for medium- to high-humidity plants. A shallow tray is filled with gravel or a support grid, then filled with water. Potted plants sit on top of the gravel or the grid. Or the reservoir may be filled with moistened moss. Again, in an uncovered open space humidity trays will not have much—or any—impact on surrounding relative humidity. That said, there are certain humidity divas, such as my miniature prayer plant, that I do sit on top of a pebble tray as, anecdotally, I find it helps even in an open area. In a Wardian case or under a glass cloche, pebble trays will increase humidity.

Growing under glass

Tiny plants that require higher humidity than an indoor windowsill environment can provide can be grown under glass in a Wardian case, cloche, glass vessel with a lid, or planted in a terrarium. The great thing about keeping high humidity plants under glass is that you will not have to water them very often, making them relatively low maintenance specimens. Growing under glass is also handy if you are going to be away from home for a while; you will not have to worry about tiny plant babies drying out while you are gone. A cloche or glass case can immediately turn a high-maintenance, high-humidity plant specimen into a very low-maintenance plant companion.

Cloche

A cloche, or bell jar, is a small glass or other transparent cover used for protecting or forcing outdoor plants or providing higher humidity to indoor plants. Think of them as humidity domes. Small cloches help maintain high-humidity specimens outside of a terrarium. I recommend placing a small tray or plate under the plant and cloche so that moisture does not build up on furniture surfaces or windowsills.

While you can certainly invest in a nice glass cloche for tiny humidity-loving plants, you need not get fancy or spend a lot of money. Keep things simple and inexpensive by using an overturned drinking glass or canning jar.

When propagating cuttings or seedlings, you can also use cloches over small germination or rooting pots. Use an overturned glass jar or drinking glass to cover up stem or leaf cuttings to speed up the rooting process.

You can even use cloches for other houseplants that do not normally grow under glass. If you are going to be to be traveling for a week or two, cover the plant with a cloche so it does not dry out. I always do this with my miniature prayer plant if I know I won't be able to water or mist it for a few days.

↑ My tiny flowering *Sinningia pusilla* 'Itaoca' grows happily in a 1½-inch (4 cm) pot under this small cloche.

↖ Some cloches have small vent holes or a wider vent hole at the top. Vented cloches are perfect for medium-humidity plants that need improved air circulation.

← A simple canning jar makes a fine cloche for my *Selaginella*.

Glass canisters

As mentioned, Wardian cases increase humidity around potted plants. The easiest way to create an inexpensive Wardian case for a single tiny, high-humidity plant is to use a simple glass jar or canister with a lid, such as a glass cookie jar, apothecary jar, or canning jar. Because the enclosed area is so small, I often vent the lids to provide a little air circulation.

An aquarium, or even a simple acrylic storage box, with a lid used to temporarily house potted high-humidity plants or to grow seedlings and cuttings may be referred to as a sweat box. Layer an inch (2.5 cm) or so of potting soil or moss in the bottom to hold extra moisture and simply set potted plants on top.

To prevent decay, be sure to remove spent flowers and foliage from plants grown under glass. Tiny plants often have tiny, delicate root systems and structures. Rather than trying to remove spent foliage or flowers with your fingers—which could pull the entire plant from its pot—I suggest getting a quality pair of sharp snips for plant grooming.

↑ My potted *Lemmaphyllum microphyllum* fern grows happily in an egg-shaped glass vessel that functions as a miniature Wardian case.

← A lovely round cloche covers my *Peperomia quadrangularis* while it roots.

↑ I never hand-pinch spent flowers or leaves from my tiny sinningia. Always use clean, sharp snips!

Feed Your Tiny Plants

I am the first to admit I am lazy when it comes to fertilizing my plants. As a professional, I tend to have a "survival of the fittest" approach to gardening and houseplants. Luckily, most indoor plants, especially tiny plants, do not need much feeding to stay happy.

For the same reasons you should avoid using tap water on tiny houseplants, you may also want to avoid synthetic plant fertilizers. That is not to say there are not many effective ones available. Plant roots or leaves can take up the nutrients and minerals (salts) in synthetic fertilizers right away; however, these salts can also build up in potting soil and damage plants. Tiny plants grow in tiny containers, so toxic build-up can happen quickly.

It is also easy to overfertilize and burn plant leaves and roots with "hot" high-nitrogen synthetic fertilizers. Mixing in synthetic, granular fertilizers coated for slow release or sprinkling them on top of potting soil reduces the chance of burning your plant, but it's still very easy to overdo it. Always read the label instructions to mix and apply accordingly. When growing tiny plants, it's advisable to not use more than quarter strength of the recommended application strength of synthetic fertilizers, be they granular or liquid.

Personally, I feed my houseplants—especially the tiny ones—with natural liquid fertilizers that contain ingredients such as liquid humus, seaweed, and fish emulsion. Always diluted to quarter strength (unless otherwise noted in the plant descriptions here). Many brands of organic liquid fertilizers combine these ingredients and many others. Look for a "balanced" fertilizer with an even ratio of nutrients. With an organic fertilizer, there is less risk of burning plants.

You can also mist medium- and high-humidity plants with diluted fertilizer as a foliar feed. I do not recommend misting or foliar feeding succulents, cacti, or plants with fuzzy or hairy leaves.

Some species, such as *Sinningia*, are particularly sensitive to fertilizers. I have killed or damaged several of mine simply by applying a small amount of liquid fertilizer that was not adequately diluted. Some species, such as many carnivorous plants, do not need to be fertilized.

FERTILIZER TIP Apply a quarter-strength dilution of liquid fertilizer no more than once per month during the plant's active growing season.

← I keep natural liquid fertilizer in small dropper bottles so I can easily add it to my squeeze and spray bottles.

Light Your Tiny Plants

Light for indoor plants is one of the most confusing topics for new and experienced plant keepers alike. Typically, plants are grouped into general categories, such as high, medium, or low light. Bright diffuse or indirect light is the go-to description for light needs for most indoor plants. But what does that mean?

LIGHT LEVELS

In general, bright diffuse, or bright indirect, light means the space looks bright to your eye, but plants are not getting hit with direct sun rays. However, when measured, "bright diffuse light" indoors often equates to low light (filtered shade) in the natural outdoor environment.

Low to medium light levels suit most foliage tropicals and many of the tiny plants in this book. Full sun plants, such as many succulents and cacti, require direct sunlight or more hours of light with grow lights.

Generally speaking, windowsill exposure can help estimate plant placement. While ultimately it is the accumulated total of light volume through the day (Daily Light Integral = DLI) that truly matters for your plants, there is a difference in the intensity of direct sunlight from different exposures (see page 171).

In the northern hemisphere, unobstructed southern windows typically receive the highest light volume and are best for high-light plants; but there may be too much direct sun, which can burn low or medium light plants. Move a foot or two (30 to 60 cm) away from a southern window and you may find it suitable for most houseplants. East facing windows are often the best location for most medium light or part sun plants, and for most houseplants in general. Morning sunlight is generally less intense than afternoon sun. West facing exposures will sustain many medium light plants and succulents and cacti that can handle a few hours of direct hot sun rays. North facing windows offer the lowest light volume, especially if there are any roof overhangs or obstructions; this exposure is best reserved for very low light plants; or the addition of supplemental grow lighting. The opposite is true in the southern hemisphere.

Light intensity and hours of light in each exposure is also much different depending on the seasons; higher in summer, lower in winter.

There is a difference between a plant thriving or surviving. Many plants tolerate a wide range of light conditions and can survive in lower than ideal light levels; they just may not grow vigorously and may be more easily overwatered. Many flowering species, such African violets, grow fine in low light, but may not flower. Don't assume plants that can tolerate low light will either live up to your expectations under such conditions or thrive indefinitely. If a plant is getting spindly and looks like it's in decline, move it to a location with more light or add a grow light.

GENERAL LIGHT CATEGORIES

I have equated general light categories for a few sample plant genera, with average DLI ranges. Plants can typically tolerate higher or lower than ideal light levels, with varied performance; most plants will cross over into more than one light category.

LIGHT CATEGORY	OUTDOOR CONDITIONS	DIRECT SUN	AVERAGE DLI	EXAMPLE GENERA
High light (unobstructed southern exposure)	Full sun	6–8 hours	18–30 mol/m2/d	*Aloe, Cattleya, Cephalotus, Dendrobium, Drosera, Echeveria, Ficus lyrata, Lithops,* many succulents and cacti, *Primula, Sedum, Senecio, Schefflera, Vanda*
Medium light (east or west exposure)	Part sun/part shade	3–4 hours	11–16 mol/m2/d	*Begonia, Bromeliads, Dracaena, Haworthia,* large *Sinningia,* succulent *Peperomia, Pinguicula, Streptocarpus, Utricularia*
Low light (east or northeast exposure)	Filtered bright shade	Dappled sunlight, high tree canopy	6–10 mol/m2/d	*Aglaonema, Anubias, Dracula,* many *Gloxinia,* many ferns, *Ludisia,* many foliage plants, *Masdevallia, Monstera,* micro *Peperomia, Phalaenopsis, Saintpaulia,* micro *Sinningia, Syngonium*
Very low light (north exposure or room interior)	Heavy shade	No direct sun, dense/low canopy	3–6 mol/m2/d	Many ferns and fern allies, *Epipremnum, Maranta,* mosses, *Philodendron, Selaginella, Spathiphyllum, Zamioculcas*

Estimate Natural Light

Accurate light measurements matter and understanding DLI is the magic key to successful indoor grow lighting. That said, I assure you general light categories are still useful as a house-plant grower. As with any learned skill, given time and hands-on experience, you will be able to better "eyeball" and intuit how high, medium, or low light levels naturally manifest in your home and which plants work in which areas. Having some failures and successes with different types of plants in different locations will help you learn about natural light availability. It just takes practice.

A simple technique for gauging natural ambient light levels without using any fancy tools is to use indicator plants. If you think you have a high-light location, try placing a full sun succulent, such as an echeveria or sedum, in this area for a few weeks. Observe its health and performance. If it does not begin to grow and thrive in this location—if stems begin to stretch and leaves grow pale—there is not enough light. Move it to a brighter location to see if it improves.

Conversely, use a low light plant, such as a fern, to indicate high light/direct sun to medium light conditions. If leaves fade or scorch, then it is not a good spot for low light plants. If plants are happy, then use these areas for low light or deep shade plants. For more technical information on determining light levels for plants, see Measuring Light on page 171.

Artificial Grow Lighting

Unfortunately, I am not blessed with high natural light levels in my current home. Most of my windows face north with a roof overhang obstruction. Low and very low light plants occupy these spots. I provide supplemental grow lighting for plants throughout my home, even for plants on my windowsills. When it comes to many of the tiny plants in this book—especially the succulents and flowering plants—I grow most on shelves with grow lighting, in lighted terrariums, or in the interior of a room with a nicer-looking grow light.

The great thing about tiny plants is that you do not need big grow lights to keep lots of them happy! Small spotlight or bar grow lights can maintain tiny plants in any location. You can even use LED or CFL grow lamps (bulbs) with an E26 or E27 base in a variety of standard home light fixtures. Both types are mechanically interchangeable, but you must always ensure the voltage is compatible with your light fixture. E27 bulbs are typically safe to use in E26 light fixtures, but it's best to avoid using E26 bulbs in E27 light fixtures.

Full spectrum HO T5 fluorescent and LED grow lights are the most useful for growing tiny plants. While lamp wattage does not determine the quality of light output from a given lamp,

← You can install adjustable LED grow lights in bookshelves or under counters. On the left bookcase I have a collection of ferns that receive low light levels (shade/dappled shade) for 8 hours per day. On the right shelf, I have flowering specimens that receive medium (part sun/part shade) light levels for 12 hours per day.

← ↑ Small, attractive LED grow shelves, such as these units that can be hung on a wall or stacked on tables, are perfect for growing collections of tiny plants.

OPPOSITE PAGE: Use small, directional LED grow lights to provide supplemental light for tiny plants around your living spaces.

you can use basic power ranges to determine usefulness for both types and size of plant material. For example, a small 9-watt grow lamp bulb will only provide a little supplemental light for a single standard size houseplant, but it could sustain a few tiny plants in a small footprint. If you need to add supplemental light to a windowsill garden or to light a group of tiny plants, look for a 20- to 40-watt bulb instead. A 40-watt grow lamp will be able to light a shelf's worth of small succulents or help sustain a larger medium-light foliage houseplant. But this is just a generalization.

Light Impacts Watering

It is especially important to understand the relationship between light and water use in plants. When plants accumulate less light, the rate of photosynthesis and transpiration slows. That means they cannot use the water at the root zone as fast as they would with more light volume. Overwatering succulents in low light conditions is extremely easy to do and is the most common reason new plant parents struggle with indoor succulents. Move plants to a high light area and they will be able to take up water more quickly from the soil.

How long should you run indoor grow lights? That depends on the type of lamp, the plant species, and ambient light. Running grow lights for 12 to 14 hours per day typically provides the equivalent of natural outdoor light requirements (again, depending on the lamp).

Because plants quantify light accumulation over time, increase the DLI delivered by either shortening or lengthening the time you run the grow light. Using the same grow lamp, you could grow a shade plant by running the light for 6 to 8 hours in a room with ambient light or a full sun plant by running the grow light for 12 to 14 hours.

If you have medium ambient light levels, and are supplementing the natural light in a space with grow lights, run them for shorter durations—a few hours—to give plants a boost. If you are relying on grow lights to provide *all* the available light for tiny plants (such as in a windowless room or closed grow tent), make sure to run grow lights for no less than 10 hours, and ideally 16 to 18 hours, per day to deliver enough light, depending on the species.

General recommendation: For groups of tiny plants, estimate a 20W grow lamp for every 2 ft² (1,858 cm²) of growing space.

← A full spectrum 20W LED grow lamp gives these succulents the supplemental light they need to be healthy.

The closer you place a plant to a light source, the more light volume it receives. Sun loving plants and seedlings can be placed closer to a grow lamp. Many full sun flowering plants can be placed fewer than 12 inches (30 cm) from a grow lamp. To reduce light volume levels for medium or low light plants, raise the grow lamp up higher above the plants. Plants will tell you quickly if they are too close (faded color or burning) or too far from the grow lamp (stretching or not flowering).

To take a deep dive into grow lighting, read my book, *Gardening Under Lights: The Complete Guide for Indoor Growers.*

Propagate Tiny Plants

Once you start collecting tiny plants, you are bound to get bitten by the propagation bug. Making more of the plants you love is almost irresistible! Each species will have its own unique requirements and environmental conditions for propagation, as well as limitations on how it can be propagated. Keep in mind that hybrid cultivars will not come true from seed, and it is not legal to propagate cultivars that are patented.

ASEXUAL REPRODUCTION

Many tiny plants can be multiplied using asexual vegetative propagation techniques, also called cloning. Taking a stem cutting of an easy houseplant, such as pothos ivy, or offset of a spider plant and rooting it in water is often a new plant parent's first foray into vegetative propagation. Getting a new cutting to root before it rots is always the goal. The sooner rooting occurs, the better chance the cutting will be successful.

Vegetative cloning involves taking a piece of tissue from a "mother plant" that can grow both new roots and bud shoots. Always choose a healthy mother plant from which to take a cutting or divide a new plantlet. Types of vegetative propagation often used include:

* Stem tip cuttings
* Leaf bud stem cuttings
* Whole leaf cuttings
* Leaf petiole cuttings
* Split-vein cuttings

* Rhizome cuttings
* Tuber or corm division
* Bulb division
* Pups and offsets
* Clump division

Stem and leaf cuttings are the most common methods for propagating tiny plants. You can root many stem and leaf cuttings directly in clean water, but there are also many other viable substrates. I typically recommend using an inert media (no organic matter) to help prevent disease and decay. Materials such as moist sphagnum moss, coir, rockwool, Oasis cubes, Leca, or a sterile potting mix are ideal.

Cover tropical cuttings with a humidity dome or cloche or place the cutting inside a glass jar to increase humidity and speed up rooting. You can also use rooting hormone on stem cuttings to accelerate root formation. When water rooting, always use clean water (purified is best) and change it at least weekly.

You can root vegetative cuttings in low light, with no grow lights needed; natural light levels in your home are adequate until new leaf buds begin growing.

Another fascinating part from which plants can clone themselves is a gemma. Gemmae are asexual budlike propagules—modified leaf structures—that can develop into an entirely new clone plant. Collect mature gemmae and germinate them just like you would seed. Pygmy sundews and butterworts, which I introduce in this book, produce gemmae, as do mosses and liverworts, as well as fungi and algae.

↑ Leaf petiole cuttings of sinningia and begonias water rooting; see the callus and new roots developed on the cutting.

← A tip stem cutting of a heart leaf philodenron rooting in water will slowly grow roots of its own.

↑ When taking a tip stem cutting, as from this *Marcgravia umbellata*, it's important to use clean, sharp snips.

↑ I made several cuttings from this piece. Aerial root initials are starting along the stem.

↑ Rooting the stem cuttings on moist sphagnum moss in a covered glass canister is an effective propagation strategy.

This water-rooted begonia leaf petiole cutting is growing new bud shoots.

These whole leaf cuttings of *Echeveria* are developing new roots and bud shoots. You do not need to cover succulent cuttings or use humidity domes for succulents.

Peperomia prostrata stem cuttings quickly root under the higher humidity conditions under glass.

String of pearls can be propagated using stem cuttings, division, or seeds.

This leaf petiole cutting of a miniature African violet is rooting in a moist soilless mix.

Thimble cactus is most easily propagated by rooting the small offsets.

A new flush of roots is growing on this sinningia tip stem cutting rooted in sphagnum moss under glass.

Pups at the base of *Graptopetalum rusbyi* (*Echeveria rusbyi*) can be cut away from the mother plant and potted up.

SEXUAL REPRODUCTION

Flowering species can reproduce sexually via seeds. While many of the tiny plant species featured do flower, the seeds they set are so tiny (almost microscopic) that it can make successful collection and germination a challenge. Even so, getting a tiny species to grow from seed is particularly rewarding.

Producing flowers and seeds takes a lot of energy, which is why flowering plants typically need more light than foliage plants or non-flowering species. Seeds of a species will come true, meaning when the seeds collected from the plant germinate, the seedlings will have the same characteristics as the mother plant.

When plants naturally hybridize or are manually cross pollinated with other closely related species, varieties, or genera, the seeds collected will not come true. The seedlings you collect and grow from a hybrid cultivar or variety will have varied characteristics of either or both parent species. Some hybrids are sterile, meaning they will not produce viable seed. If you wish to clone a hybrid cultivar, you must use a viable form of vegetative propagation.

While some tiny bloomers produce seed that is easy to collect, others have specific pollination requirements that can be difficult to reproduce; or produce seed that is so tiny it can be challenging to collect. Some seeds will germinate easily with no special preparation, while others—often from succulents or cacti—may require special scarification or stratification preparation techniques to successfully germinate.

African violets, for example, require you to hand pollinate the female flowers with pollen from the male flowers to set seed. If seed set is successful, the seed pod will then need to remain on the plant for four to six months to mature. If you can collect the nearly microscopic seeds after that, they will need exposure to light to germinate successfully. It can be quite the complicated process, tricky even for experienced growers. And remember, only seed from a species or naturally occurring variety will come true. Seedlings from hybrids will be random variations. Luckily, African violets propagate very easily using several methods of vegetative cloning.

← I love starting seeds of tiny living stones and other succulents, because the baby seedlings are just so adorable!

→ Vietnamese violet (*Primulina tamiana*) produces a profusion of relatively large and easy-to-collect seeds. As this is a species, seedlings will come true.

Each species has its own special requirements for both seed set and germination. In general, germinating seeds require a high volume of light and will need grow lights placed several inches over the containers to be run for 14 to 16 hours per day. Once seedlings have grown their first set of true leaves, begin raising the grow lights to avoid burning the plants. Transplant to a new container once seedlings have rooted out to fill the root plug or container.

Certain non-flowering plants, such as ferns, liverworts, mosses, and algae, produce spores instead of seeds. The sporangia on the undersides of ferns release spores, which grow into heart-shaped gametophytes called prothalli if they are lucky enough to germinate. An individual prothallus grows female and male sex organs and produces both male and female gametes—egg and sperm. Once released, the sperm swims to fertilize the egg. The resulting zygote grows into an embryo and then a mature fern plant before starting the cycle over again. Collect spores and germinate them to grow your own baby ferns, but be aware that the sperm need enough moisture to make the swim to the egg.

To learn all the fundamental of plant propagation and many techniques for both vegetative propagation and seed starting, be sure to read my book, *Plant Parenting: Easy Ways to Make More Houseplants, Vegetables, and Flowers*.

↑ Seeds from my tiny *Sinningia pusilla* 'Itaoca' are the size of specks of dust! This is a naturally occurring variety of the parent species that will come true from seed.

→ Rust-colored sori (clusters of sporangia) dot the undersides of my *Lemmaphyllum microphyllum* fern. Germinate mature spores or simply take rhizome cuttings to propagate a fern vegetatively.

3

tiny windowsill plants

TINY WINDOWSILL PLANTS thrive in normal home humidity and temperature levels. While some species may appreciate a bit of misting now and then, especially if your house is very dry, you can place these petite plants anywhere in your home where light levels are appropriate for the species. Tiny windowsill plants are also good choices for an office environment where artificial light is available, and they fit perfectly tucked into a corner on a desk.

Many of the tropical plants that can thrive on a windowsill may also be appropriate for growing in a terrarium or under glass. Just keep in mind that soggy root systems will not make most of these plants happy. Make sure to provide good drainage and air circulation for these species.

> *Be sure to explore the "Grow the Same Way" sections for suggestions of many more tiny windowsill plants you can collect and grow under relatively similar conditions.*

→ One of my favorite minature ferns, *Nephrolepis exaltata* 'Fluffy Ruffles'.

Foliage

With the boom in popularity of aroids and foliage plants, I know plant parents will be fascinated to discover some miniature versions they can add to their collection, especially if space has become scarce due to bigger potted foliage plants.

Most truly tiny windowsill plants that can tolerate low humidity fall into the succulent category. The tiniest of tropical foliage plants tend to need high humidity and are best suited to growing under glass or will require regular misting. That said, a few tiny tropical foliage specimens can thrive out in the open in small pots on your windowsill or desk.

When it comes to miniature tropical foliage windowsill plants, their "tiny" designation is often relative to the size of more common parent or related species.

← A few of my assorted tiny windowsill plants grow in 2-inch (5 cm) pots.

BULL'S EYE BEGONIA

Most houseplant keepers do a double take at this plant, inadvertently confusing it with the popular *Pilea peperomioides* or a species of peperomia. Not so! While this diminutive begonia does resemble these unrelated plant species, it is a unique species with a more succulent look than most begonias. The fleshy, shiny shell-shaped leaves sport a distinct red dot where the petiole attaches to the leaf. The fragrant flowers, produced in late-winter and early spring, are white and are borne on peduncles that rise 1 to 2 inches (5 to 8 cm) above the foliage. This species of begonia grows naturally in the rainforests of Costa Rica, El Salvador, and Panama.

Size Plants grow with a creeping rhizome, producing 1- to 2-inch (2.5 to 5 cm) leaves that vary in height from 5 to 8 inches (13 to 20 cm) tall. My plant, grown in a 3-inch (8 cm) planter, tends to stay under 6 inches (15 cm) tall.

Care Bull's Eye begonia does nicely in a low to medium indoor light location, equivalent to part shade. Plants can handle an east-facing window exposure, but if there is too much direct sun, move it away from the windowsill. You can also grow under low intensity grow lights to provide medium light conditions.

These plants need thorough waterings but, like most rhizomatous begonias, prefer to dry a bit in between. If plants are left to sit soggy, they can quickly rot. Use lukewarm water, never cold; bottom watering is often best. Plant in a porous clay pot to provide good root aeration.

While plants can thrive in 60 to 80 percent humidity with good air circulation, they also do fine in normal home conditions. Like many begonias, Bull's Eye will grow nicely as a potted plant on an open windowsill or set or planted into an open bubble bowl or open terrarium.

PLANT TYPE · Terrestrial

SKILL LEVEL · Easy to intermediate

LIGHT · Medium, no direct sun

SOIL · Loose, well-draining

MOISTURE · Frequent watering, allow to dry slightly

HUMIDITY · Medium to high

TEMPERATURE · Warm, 50°F to 86°F (10°C to 30°C)

FERTILIZER · Monthly spring through fall at quarter strength

SIZE · 5 to 8 inches (13 to 20 cm) tall and wide

PROPAGATION · Whole leaf cuttings, leaf petiole cuttings, rhizome cuttings, seed

GROW THE SAME WAY
Begonia foliosa,
B. hydrocotylifolia,
B. ningmingensis 'Bella'

← This Bull's Eye begonia is happy growing in a 2-inch (5 cm) clay planter.

MINIATURE PRAYER PLANT,
HERRINGBONE PLANT

P rayer plants have captured the hearts of plant parents everywhere. The uniquely patterned leaves, which open and close with light and dark cycles, always fascinate. Although there are forty to fifty different species of prayer plant, market availability is often limited to *Maranta leuconeura* and species of the closely related *Calathea*. Miniature prayer plant, *M. repens,* looks just like its bigger cousins with the classic rabbit tracks pattern on pale, moss green leaves. Perfect for tucking into a smaller windowsill or place on your desk, plants occasionally produce small mauve flowers. Miniature prayer plant is native to the warm tropical areas of Central and South America and the West Indies. Plants grow in rhizomatous clumps in moist swampy conditions.

Size *M. repens* typically grow to about 5 inches (13 cm) tall and can reach about 12 inches (30 cm) wide—or long as they trail. Mature leaves are typically 3 to 4 inches (8 to 10 cm) long.

Care Prayer plants have a reputation for being a little finicky as houseplants. They grow fine in low light but may be more vigorous in medium light. Choose a north facing windowsill or similar light exposure or an eastern exposure if plants need a boost. Leaves fade in color if plants are getting too much light. Maranta need to be constantly moist but also need good drainage; do not let plants sit in water. Mist plants daily or use a humidity tray if curling or brown leaf tips indicate more humidity is needed.

Plants have shallow roots. If you are struggling with maranta, switch to a wider, shorter planter to help better manage the moisture at the root zone. Miniature prayer plant is a good candidate for small hanging planters or wall planters that allow them to cascade. Miniature maranta will thrive on your windowsill with consistent root moisture but are also petite enough to grow under a glass cloche or planted in a terrarium with *good* drainage.

PLANT TYPE · Terrestrial, rhizomatous

SKILL LEVEL · Easy to intermediate

LIGHT · Low to medium, no direct sun

SOIL · Loose, well-draining

MOISTURE · Frequent watering, consistently moist but not soggy

HUMIDITY · Medium to high

TEMPERATURE · Warm, 68°F to 80°F (20°C to 27°C)

FERTILIZER · Monthly spring through fall at quarter strength

SIZE · 5 inches (13 cm) tall

PROPAGATION · Rhizome cuttings, stem cuttings, root division

GROW THE SAME WAY
Calathea 'Dottie', *Lusidia discolor, Macodes petola*

← My miniature prayer plant grows in a 2-inch (5 cm) container.

GOLD VEINED SHAMROCK

O xalis are a fascinating group of plants we are most accustomed to seeing in the outdoor garden, but they easily transition indoors. Commonly called false shamrocks (*Trifolium repens* is the real shamrock), there are many beautiful small oxalis species. Gold veined shamrock is a favorite of mine, for both its striking yellow to orange veins and ease of care. While I grow it for the foliage, plants do produce tubular pink flowers. It is a perfect little windowsill or desk plant companion. Leaves close after two hours in darkness, then unfold in the light! This species is originally native to South America but has spread to all continents except Antarctica.

Size Plants typically reach to 6 inches (15 cm) tall when grown indoors. Brighter light tends to keep plants more compact, at about 4 inches (10 cm) tall, with flowers a little taller than the foliage. Bulbs will multiply and plants will eventually fill the container, creating a wider specimen.

Care Plants are bulbous, and they can sometimes go dormant in summer months if temperatures are hot. However, indoors they typically remain evergreen. Plants enjoy bright, indirect light in an eastern or southern windowsill, but if it looks like foliage is scorching, move it away from the window or lower the light exposure. Plants can grow under small LED grow lights placed a couple of feet overhead, but lamps that run too hot could send oxalis into dormancy.

Make sure pots have good drainage, and keep plants evenly moist. While you do not want to overwater gold veined shamrock, its thin delicate leaf petioles do not hold a lot of water, so they will quickly wilt if they are too dry. Once watered, they will perk back up. If plants wilt regularly, pot up into a slightly larger, non-porous container.

PLANT TYPE · Terrestrial, bulb

SKILL LEVEL · Easy

LIGHT · Medium, no direct sun

SOIL · Well-draining

MOISTURE · Consistently moist, not soggy

HUMIDITY · Low to medium

TEMPERATURE · Warm, 50°F to 85°F (10°C to 30° C)

FERTILIZER · Monthly at quarter strength

SIZE · 4 to 6 inches (10 to 15 cm) tall

PROPAGATION · Division of bulbs, leaf-petiole cutting

GROW THE SAME WAY *Oxalis bullulata, O. hedysaroides, O. minuta, O. spiralis, O. vulcanicola* and its varieties and hybrids.

← This gold veined shamrock grows in a tiny, 1½-inch (4 cm) handmade planter.

CREEPING BUTTON FERN

reeping button fern is one of the few teeny-tiny ferns that is perfectly happy growing in the open on a windowsill. No terrarium or misting required! Its fuzzy foliage is particularly delightful. The small leaves are light green and covered with a rust-colored pubescence along the long, creeping rhizomes. Creeping button fern originates in tropical forests of Southeast Asia and Indonesia, typically creeping along tree trunks and growing alongside orchids and mosses.

Size Plant height typically stays under 2 to 3 inches (10 cm), though the creeping rhizomes may reach 6 to 10 inches (15 to 25 cm). Leaves measure between ½ to 1 inch (1 to 2.5 cm) long. My specimens grow happily in small 2- to 3-inch (5 to 8 cm) pots. The creeping rhizomes can stretch to a whopping 40 inches (100 cm) in their natural environment if the plant has nearby tree trunks or other supports on which to grow.

Care If you struggle with ferns give this easy one a try, as it is tolerant of a variety of growing conditions. Creeping button fern does best in medium light levels but can tolerate low light. No direct sun! An east-facing window is ideal, as is a foot or so away from a southern exposure. I also grow it under LED grow lights (at least a couple feet [.5 m] away from plants). A north window may also do, but increase the light volume if plants do not put on new growth.

Creeping button fern can tolerate some drying between waterings but prefers consistent moisture, as do most ferns. Grow this semi-epiphytic fern potted up in small, non-porous planters with a loose potting mix (preferably mixed with coir). It can be planted directly into a terrarium or planted into a bubble bowl if conditions are not soggy. Vines will attach and grow on bark or other supports. Feed plants monthly at quarter strength with a liquid humus fertilizer.

PLANT TYPE · Hemiepiphyte

SKILL LEVEL · Easy

LIGHT · Medium

SOIL · Loose, well-draining coir mix, chopped moss, tree fern support, bark

MOISTURE · Consistently moist, can tolerate some drying

HUMIDITY · Medium to high

TEMPERATURE · Warm, 68°F to 85°F (20°C to 30° C)

FERTILIZER · Monthly or bi-monthly, spring through fall at quarter to half strength

SIZE · 3 inches (8 cm) tall by 12 inches (31 cm) wide

PROPAGATION · Rhizome cuttings, clump division, spores

GROW THE SAME WAY
Nephrolepis exaltata 'Fluffy Ruffles', *Pellaea rotundifolia*, *Pyrrosia* spp.

← Creeping button fern growing in a glazed 2½-inch (6 cm) pot is cute as a button.

Syngonium podophyllum

'MINI PIXIE', DWARF ARROWHEAD PLANT

When I discovered this micro-miniature arrowhead plant, my mind was a little bit blown. It is the *cutest* little houseplant. 'Mini Pixie' looks just like any standard juvenile arrowhead plant but with heart-shaped leaves the size of your fingernail. Creamy white variegated centers accent the leaves. The species is native to Latin America, ranging from Mexico to Bolivia. However, plants have naturalized in the southern continental U.S. and Hawaii, as well as the West Indies. Juvenile plants grow in a contained clump. As plants mature, stems begin to elongate, produce aerial roots, and creep along the ground or climb up neighboring plants or other supports.

Size 'Mini Pixie' typically stays in a clump form only 2 to 3 inches (5 to 8 cm) tall and wide. It can produce tiny running stems as it matures, but it is less apt to do so than its parent *Syngonium* species. The tiny heart-shaped leaves measure ½ to ¾ of an inch (1.2 to 1.9 cm).

Care *Syngonium* 'Mini Pixie' is a versatile little aroid you can grow in varying conditions. Plants have low to medium indirect light needs and prefer the equivalent of an east-facing window but will tolerate lower and higher light levels. More light will keep plants more compact; less light will result in a more elongated clump.

Plants do well in normal home humidity levels. If the leaf edges seem to be drying a bit due to low humidity, mist the foliage a few times per week. Plants grow happily in 2- to 3-inch (5 to 8 cm) pots with several waterings per week. While they like moisture, syngonium do not like "wet feet," so use a lightweight potting mix for indoor plants and consider adding some coir to keep moisture more uniform. Plants can dry a bit between waterings on your windowsill; however, you also can plant 'Mini Pixie' and other mini syngonium into terrariums.

PLANT TYPE · Hemiepiphyte

SKILL LEVEL · Easy

LIGHT · Low to medium, no direct sun

SOIL · Loose, well-draining

MOISTURE · Frequent watering, consistently moist but not soggy

HUMIDITY · Medium

TEMPERATURE · Warm, 68°F to 80°F (20°C to 27°C)

FERTILIZER · Monthly, spring through fall at quarter strength

SIZE · 3 inches (8 cm) tall

PROPAGATION · Stem cuttings with node/aerial root, clump division

GROW THE SAME WAY *Syngonium* 'Mini Allusion', S. 'Pink Pixie', *Nephrolepis exaltata* 'Mini Russell's', *N. exaltata* 'Fluffy Ruffles'

← The leaves of *Syngonium podophyllum* 'Mini Pixie' are smaller than your fingertips!

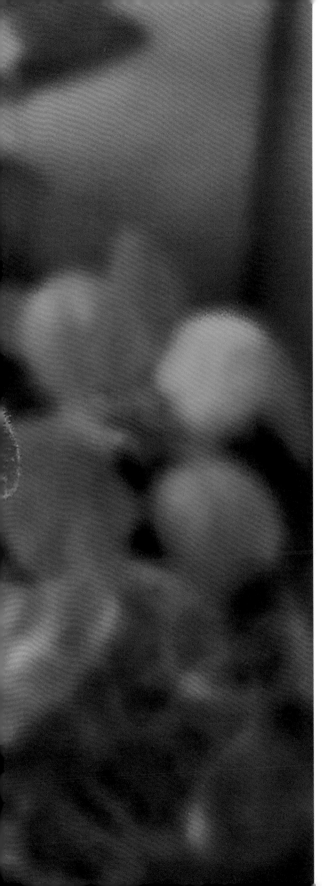

Flowering

Most plant parents stick to foliage plants indoors because blooming plants can seem trickier to grow or need too much light. However, there are certain tiny bloomers well-suited to indoor growing conditions, especially if you provide supplemental grow lighting.

Many of my favorite tiny bloomers hail from the gesneriad category. Gesneriads as a group include plants such as African violets, gloxinia, and cape primrose. Many tiny succulents also put on impressive blooms; however, most succulents are primarily grown for their foliage.

Micro orchids are the pinnacle of my tiny plant obsession. There are thousands of miniature and micro orchids to add to your collection, with an abundance to choose from available in the plant trade. That said, micro orchids can be tricky to grow for beginners. Many micro orchids are recommended for growing inside terrariums, as they need consistent moisture around their aerial roots and higher relative humidity. However, beginners may find terrarium conditions a bit challenging, and many tiny orchids can quickly rot from excess moisture and inadequate aeration. The micro-orchid species listed here in the windowsill section *can* be grown in terrariums or orchidariums, but they are also tolerant of open environment culture.

← Miniature African violet 'Rob's Wascally Wabbit'

One of my very favorite tiny bloomers, Vietnamese violet packs big flower power into a tiny space year-round. I adore the small, fuzzy oval leaves of this miniature gesneriad, which emerge in clusters of small rosettes. Two striking dark purple stripes accent the pure white tubular flowers. As a bonus, plants produce plenty of seed. You will be hard pressed to not succumb to this tiny plant's easy charm. Vietnamese violet is native to China and North Vietnam.

Size The foliage of Vietnamese violet typically grows to a maximum height of 3 inches (8 cm), with flower stems reaching 5 to 6 inches (13 to 15 cm) tall. Plants will quite happily reside in 2- to 3-inch (5 to 8 cm) pots, even pot bound.

Care Vietnamese violets are often easier to care for than their African violet cousins, and bloom more consistently, in my experience. Plants need medium light levels for good flowering, but no direct sunlight. Choose an east-facing windowsill or grow it on a shelf under grow lights as you would an African violet. If plants are not flowering, increase the light volume. Plants tend to like it a bit on the cooler side, so favor LEDs over other types of grow lights. It is a perfect desk plant in an office with bright artificial lighting.

Plants prefer consistent moisture, but never soggy. Make sure containers have a drainage hole; a porous container can help. Bottom watering is best. While plants can handle higher humidity when kept in a glass case, they do not require it, and it is best to keep water off the fuzzy foliage. Plants can be repotted once per year, which may eliminate the need to fertilize these light feeders. Use an African violet potting mix when repotting. Plants will seed freely, but if you want plants to flower more, deadhead the spent flowers before they go to seed.

PLANT TYPE · Terrestrial

SKILL LEVEL · Easy

LIGHT · Low to medium, no direct sun

SOIL · Loose, well-draining

MOISTURE · Consistently moist, not soggy

HUMIDITY · Medium

TEMPERATURE · Cool to warm, 50°F to 80°F (10°C to 27°C)

FERTILIZER · African violet food 2 to 3 times per year at half to quarter strength

SIZE · 3 to 6 inches (8 to 15 cm) tall

PROPAGATION · Seed, stem cutting, leaf petiole cutting, division

GROW THE SAME WAY *Codonanthe devosiana, Primulina* spp., *Streptocarpus* spp., African violets

---

← Seeds are developing from some spent blooms on the Vietnamese violet growing in this 2½-inch (6 cm) pot, and there are many more bloom spikes on the way!

Primulina × hybrida 'Piccolo'

ASIAN VIOLET

P rimulina, which used to be included in the now defunct genus Chirita, are a lovely group of compact yet impressive bloomers. *Primulina* 'Piccolo' grows in a tight rosette form with dark, thick leaves, often with a variegated pattern. Plants bloom almost non-stop with tall sprays of large, tubular flowers emerging from the center of the plant. Flower color is intense from violet to lavender. Asian violets are found naturally growing as understory plants in high elevations in Sri Lanka and India into China, and even Sumatra, Java, and Borneo.

Size 'Piccolo' is a compact hybrid of two other Primulina species. Foliage typically stays under 2 inches (5 cm) tall with 3-inch (8 cm) leaves that fold over the pot. Plants live happily in a small, 3-inch (8 cm) container. The flowers can reach approximately 8 inches (20 cm) tall, and cascade downward.

Care If you love African violets but struggle to grow them successfully, try primulinas. They thrive in a partial sun situation in an east-facing windowsill. Think morning sun with after-noon shade. Like Vietnamese violet, plants can tolerate lower light levels, but if they stop blooming, increase light. Supplement light with grow lamps as you would with African violets; but do not let plants get too hot.

Plants thrive in low humidity but need consistent soil moisture with good drainage; never leave plants soggy. Just as with Vietnamese or African violets, plants are best bottom watered when the soil surface feels dry. Keep water off the foliage. Plants are light feeders, so you do not need to fertilize often, but to encourage blooms use a quarter- or half-strength liquid fertilizer. Repot primulina once per year using an African violet potting mix, which may reduce any need to fertilize much at all.

PLANT TYPE · Terrestrial

SKILL LEVEL · Easy

LIGHT · Medium, morning sun, afternoon shade

SOIL · Loose, well-draining

MOISTURE · Consistent, dry lightly between waterings

HUMIDITY · Low

TEMPERATURE · Cool, 50°F to 80°F (10°C to 27°C)

FERTILIZER · African violet food monthly spring through fall at quarter to half strength

SIZE · 3 inches (8 cm) tall

PROPAGATION · Leaf cuttings, stem cuttings, division, seed (seed from hybrids does not come true)

GROW THE SAME WAY *Primulina* spp., *Streptocarpus* spp.

← *Primulina* 'Piccolo' growing in a 2½-inch (6 cm) container shows off its (relatively) huge flowers.

MICROMINI AFRICAN VIOLETS

There are three recognized size categories of African violet: standard, semi-miniature, and miniature. While standard varieties and cultivars descend from the *Saintpaulia ionantha* species, the semi-miniature and miniature types result from two smaller species, *S. pusilla* and *S. shumensis*. In the 1960s, plant breeders used these two later species to create the miniature and micromini African violets found on the market today. There are about twenty known species of African violets native to the Usambara Mountains in Kenya and Nguru Mountains of Tanzania.

Size Mini African violets grow to a mature size of fewer than 6 inches (15 cm) tall and wide, while microminis mature at half this size. Leaves of some micromini African violets are less than ¼ inch (0.6 cm) long.

Care Micromini African violets can thrive in low to medium light levels, with best blooming in medium light (bright indirect indoors). A north-facing windowsill often won't get plants blooming; move to an eastern exposure. Turn plants regularly to avoid stretched, "necky" plants. You can also grow them under fluorescent or LED grow lights. If you have an office with bright artificial lighting, micromini African violets are a perfect desk plant.

Microminis should be in containers no larger than 2 inches (5 cm) wide and tall to prevent crown rot. If you tend to overwater, go even a little smaller on the container. It is best to keep soil damp with bottom watering or wick-watering, but do not let soil get or stay soggy and allow it to dry between waterings. Use Oyama or self-watering planters. Keep water off the foliage.

African violets enjoy high relative humidity levels in the 70 to 80 percent range. You *can* plant microminis in terrariums or grow them under glass if their root system is not soggy. However, they will do fine at 50 percent relative humidity in a typical home environment.

PLANT TYPE · Terrestrial

SKILL LEVEL · Easy to intermediate

LIGHT · Low to medium, no direct sun

SOIL · Loose, well-draining

MOISTURE · Consistent but never soggy; bottom water

HUMIDITY · Medium to high

TEMPERATURE · Warm, 75°F to 85°F (16°C to 30°C)

FERTILIZER · African violet food monthly spring through fall at quarter strength

SIZE · 2 to 3 inches (5 to 8 cm) tall and wide

PROPAGATION · Crown cutting, leaf cutting, split-leaf cutting, leaf petiole cutting, clump division

GROW THE SAME WAY *Petrocosmea* spp.; all *Saintpaulia* spp. varieties and cultivars, including trailing miniatures, such as 'Chantaspring'.

← This micro African violet 'Rob's Lucky Penny' is remarkable for its unusually high variegation.

Streptocarpus liliputana × 'Fernwood's Minuet'

CAPE PRIMROSE

Succulents & Cacti

Tiny succulents are some of the cutest plants you will ever grow. There are thousands from which to choose and this category could, by itself, fill many volumes. It was almost impossible for me to pick which species to highlight, so I selected a few of my favorite easy-to-grow cuties to get you started.

Most of these tiny succulents and cacti can be purchased as live plants, while more rare species are often only available as seed, or sometimes pups or stem cuttings.

Keep in mind most succulents and cacti, even tiny ones, need high light levels—akin to full to part direct sun outdoors—to thrive. The fastest way to kill succulents and cacti indoors is by overwatering in low light environments. Unless you have a big, unobstructed southern windowsill, be prepared to use grow lights to either supplement natural light or provide all the light succulents need.

← Various *Echeveria*, *Graptopetalum*, and *Mammillaria* grow in 2-inch (5 cm) pots.

CRINKLE LEAF PLANT

The chubby little pad-like leaves of crinkle leaf plant are so cute you are going to want to pinch them! This easy-to-grow succulent is perfect for beginners. The beautiful foliage emerges an emerald color but turns a lovely grey-green as leaves mature. Older leaves are covered with tiny fuzz. Another distinguishing feature is the thick coat of wiry aerial roots always present on their short stems. While grown for their foliage, plants produce small, white tubular flowers in spring or summer. Crinkle leaf plants are sun-loving succulents native to the Eastern Cape of South Africa, where plants grow in sheltered thickets and rocky outcrops.

Size *Adromischus cristatus* grows in a loose rosette form to about 6 inches (15 cm) tall but typically stays more compact in small pots.

Care Like most succulents, crinkle leaf needs high light or a full sun environment. Choose a west-facing windowsill or a bright-all-day southern windowsill. Without such windowsills, I grow my crinkle leaf plant, along with many of my other full sun succulents and cacti, 8 inches (20 cm) below two 45-watt LED grow lamps that run for 12 hours per day.

Crinkle leaf plants prefer warm, dry conditions with low humidity and a loose, well-draining soil. Use a cactus or succulent mix to repot plants, which you can do every couple of years. Like many succulents, plants will quickly rot if kept too damp. If you are an over-waterer, resist the urge with crinkle leaf plant and grow it in a smaller pot. Allow the soil to dry completely between waterings. You may only need to water plants two to four times per month during the active growing season; once per month in winter, depending on pot size, temperature, and humidity in your home.

PLANT TYPE · Terrestrial

SKILL LEVEL · Easy

LIGHT · High light, full sun

SOIL · Loose, well-draining

MOISTURE · Dry completely between waterings

HUMIDITY · Low

TEMPERATURE · Warm, 68°F to 85°F (20°C to 27°C)

FERTILIZER · Monthly, spring through fall at quarter to half strength

SIZE · 3 to 6 inches (8 to 15 cm) tall

PROPAGATION · Seed, stem cuttings, leaf cuttings, division

GROW THE SAME WAY
Adromischus cooperi, A. marianiae, Echeveria chihuahuaensis, E. globulosa, E. graptopetalum var. *filiferum, Graptopetalum rusbyi, Sedeveria* 'Blue Elf', *Sedum* spp.

← See the signature clusters of aerial roots along the main stem of this crinkle leaf plant, growing in a 2-inch (5 cm) ceramic planter.

Dracaena ehrenbergii (syn. *Sansevieria ehrenbergii*)

'SAMURAI DWARF', DWARF SNAKE PLANT

Just about every new plant parent acquires a snake plant (also called mother in law's tongue) for its ease of care and resilient nature. Snake plants are tough as nails when it comes to tolerating poor growing conditions or neglect. Most species and varieties are large; some growing 2 feet (60 cm) tall. 'Samurai Dwarf' is a miniature, yet equally sturdy, form of standard sword snake plant. These charming little troopers produce bright green cup-like pointed leaves tinged in rose gold. There is also a variegated dwarf variety. Like agaves, the tips of 'Samurai Dwarf' leaves can be a bit sharp and pokey. This dwarf variety is believed to hail from somewhere in Africa. Most sansevieria grow naturally in arid regions of Africa, Madagascar, and South Asia.

Size Plants have a short, stubby growth habit, typically growing to about 4 to 6 inches (10 to 15 cm), but some plants may grow a bit taller and wider. Leaves emerge in an alternating pattern, stacked as they grow.

Care Snake plants are probably the easiest of all houseplants in terms of care. In fact, treat snake plants like a cactus or succulent. While tolerant of low and very low light, plants look best in a medium indirect light location with no afternoon sun. A southern window exposure or east-facing window with bright morning sun does nicely.

Experts at conserving water, snake plants can dry completely and for extended periods between waterings. Always allow soil to dry completely before watering again, as soggy soil can cause plants to rot. Use a loose cactus/succulent potting mix and always use containers with drainage holes.

PLANT TYPE · Terrestrial

SKILL LEVEL · Super easy

LIGHT · Medium light, morning sun, afternoon shade

SOIL · Loose, well-draining

MOISTURE · Low to medium, allow to dry between waterings

HUMIDITY · Low

TEMPERATURE · Warm, 68°F to 80°F (20°C to 27°C)

FERTILIZER · Monthly at half strength

SIZE · 3 inches (8 cm) tall, 2- to 3-inch (5 to 8 cm) containers

PROPAGATION · Seeds, stem cuttings, clump division

GROW THE SAME WAY *Sansevieria ballyi* 'Minnie', *S. cylindrica* var. *patula* 'Boncel Dwarf', *S. pinguicula*

The genus *Sansevieria* was recently absorbed into the genus *Dracaena*, but in the marketplace, most snake plants are labeled with the old genus.

← My 'Samurai Dwarf' grows in a 3-inch (8 cm) porous planter.

BASEBALL PLANT

S o round, *so cute!* It is obvious how *Euphorbia obesa* earned it is common name, baseball plant. The plump young plants are almost perfectly round with tidy symmetrical seams. Foliage color varies from blue-green to purple with silver or copper accents, often in a striped or plaid pattern. As dioecious plants, the tiny yellow to chartreuse flowers it produces will either have stamen (male) or anthers (female). To harvest viable seed, you will need male plants to pollinate the female plants. *E. obesa* is a rare succulent native to the Great Karoo in the Eastern Cape of South Africa. Plants grow in stony, hilly areas in full sun, often partially shaded by other vegetation. While this species is endangered and protected due to overcollection in its native habitat, they are relatively widely available in cultivation.

Size Old, mature plants, especially in their native habitat, can reach a height of about 7 to 8 inches (18 to 20 cm), with a girth of up to 3 to 4 inches (8 to 10 cm). Most potted plants in cultivation stay smaller and rounder.

Care Plants need high light or full sun exposure but can tolerate some afternoon shading. Choose a bright southern window, west window, or high-output LED grow lights to keep *E. obesa* happy. I grow mine about 8 to 10 inches (25 cm) below high-output LED grow bars for 12 hours per day. You can also set them outside on a balcony or patio in a sunny spot. If the plaid-like pattern begins to fade, plants need more light.

Frequent watering is the fastest way to kill baseball plant and most other succulents. Water infrequently and allow plants to dry completely between waterings. Grow in small 2- to 4-inch (5 to 10 cm) pots to allow soil to dry more quickly. Spring through fall, water plants once per week (or less); and less frequently in winter. Plants benefit from a few seasonal feedings.

PLANT TYPE · Terrestrial

SKILL LEVEL · Easy

LIGHT · High, full morning sun, afternoon shade

SOIL · Gritty cactus mix, well-draining

MOISTURE · Sparingly, dry between waterings

HUMIDITY · Low

TEMPERATURE · Warm to hot, cool nights, 68°F to 80°F (20°C to 27°C)

FERTILIZER · 3 to 4 times spring through fall at half strength

SIZE · Up to 7 to 8 inches (17 to 20 cm) tall by 3 to 4 inches (8 to 10 cm) wide

PROPAGATION · Seed, offsets

GROW THE SAME WAY
*Euphorbia bayeri,
E. bupleurifolia, E. globosa,
E. meloformis, E. squarrosa,
Titanopsis calcarea,
T. primossii*

← Tiny anthers emerge from the blooms of my female *E. obesa* in her 2-inch-wide (5 cm) pot.

Haworthiopsis venosa ssp. *tessellata,*
(syn. *Haworthia venosa, Aloe tessellata*)

ALLIGATOR PLANT

M any cactus species are just too big, or too prickly, to keep as houseplants in tight spaces. Not so with the adorable thimble cactus! This is one of the few cacti I keep indoors as a houseplant because of its tiny size—it fits nicely under small grow lights—and manageable dense, matted spines. Plants are bright green with a narrow cylindrical body and small side branches. The tiny white spines radiate from the small tubercles in a star-like pattern. Plants often produce tiny white, bell-shaped flowers during cooler times in spring and fall. Thimble cactus grows native in the arid Hidalgo and Queretaro regions in Mexico.

Size The main stems of thimble cactus typically grow to a maximum height of about 4 inches (10 cm) and about 1 to 1¼ inches (3 cm) wide. The main stems freely produce many side branches that detach as offsets. Mature specimens will grow to a clump that can reach about 4 to 5 inches (10 to 13 cm) wide.

Care As do most cacti, thimble cactus will need high light equivalent to full or part sun conditions. Place plants in a bright southern window or west facing exposure. Or, grow with other cacti and succulents under high-output grow LED lamps placed 8 to 12 inches (20 to 30 cm) above the plants.

Overwatering indoor cacti and succulents is common, especially when light levels are too low. The tiny thimble cactus can rot, seemingly overnight, if you even think about giving it extra water—especially in winter. Allow the soil to dry completely between waterings and do not be afraid to let it stay dry for a couple of weeks. Plants will grow happily in small, 2- to 3-inch (5 to 8 cm) containers indefinitely, which can help plants dry adequately between waterings.

Handle with care! Thimble cactus is fragile, in that it's easy to knock off the small branching offsets. Simply collect any of these offsets, allow them to cure for a couple of weeks, then set them on top of soil to root new plants.

PLANT TYPE · Terrestrial

SKILL LEVEL · Easy to intermediate

LIGHT · High, full sun, tolerates afternoon shade

SOIL · Gritty cactus mix, well-draining

MOISTURE · Low, dry between waterings

HUMIDITY · Low

TEMPERATURE · Warm, 70°F to 80°F (21°C to 27°C), hardy to 14°F (-10°C)

FERTILIZER · Monthly, spring and summer at quarter strength

SIZE · 3 to 5 inches (8 to 13 cm)

PROPAGATION · Offsets, clump division, seed

GROW THE SAME WAY *Astrophytum asteria, Coryphantha vivipara, Gymnocalycium baldianum, Mammillaria candida, M. hahniana, M. zeilmanniana, Rebutia fabrisii*

← TOP: This smaller thimble cactus won't outgrow its 1-inch (2.5 cm) pot for some time.
BOTTOM RIGHT: The offsets of this mature clump of flowering thimble cactus have fallen off the mother plants.
BOTTOM LEFT: A large clump of thimble cactus grows in a 3-inch (7.5 cm) container.

ITSY BITSY PEPEROMIA

There are so many tiny peperomias to choose from, it was difficult for me to pick one succulent type to highlight for windowsills. Most of the micro peperomias need to be grown with high humidity under glass. But the succulent types, such as *Peperomia rubella*, are quite happy grown in the typical open home environment. You will fall in love with the intense pomegranate color on the underside of the leaves and stems of *P. rubella*, not to mention the striking contrasting vein patterns on the surface of the small, fat olive-colored leaves. New, young leaves are rounder with heavy white veining, and older leaves grow to a longer point. Too cute not to pinch! *P. rubella* is a miniature species native to Jamaica, where it grows as an understory plant.

Size Young plants begin by growing upright until they are 4 to 5 inches (10 to 13 cm) tall, then will cascade over the container to trail, usually to about 12 inches (30 cm) long or so.

Care Plants thrive in medium to high indirect light, but not direct hot sun. They will tolerate low light but foliage color will be less intense. Choose an east- or south-facing windowsill or grow in a north-facing window with some supplemental light. You can also grow *P. rubella* under fluorescent or LED grow lamps for 10 to 12 hours per day, but keep lamps 1 to 2 feet (30 to 60 cm) above the plants.

Even though this *P. rubella* is classified here as a succulent, it can tolerate regular watering as well as medium humidity, which is the case for most peperomia. Allow the soil to dry slightly between waterings. Grow in small, 2- to 3-inch (5 to 8 cm) pots to better manage moisture. However, itsy bitsy peperomia will also grow nicely under a cloche or in a glass case.

PLANT TYPE · Terrestrial

SKILL LEVEL · Easy

LIGHT · Medium to bright indirect light; no direct sun

SOIL · Loose, well-draining

MOISTURE · Consistent, but can dry slightly between waterings

HUMIDITY · Low to high

TEMPERATURE · Warm, 70°F to 80°F (21°C to 27°C)

FERTILIZER · Monthly at quarter strength

SIZE · 4 to 5 inches (5 to 10 cm) tall

PROPAGATION · Stem cuttings, leaf cuttings, division

GROW THE SAME WAY
Pellionia repens, Peperomia 'Pixie', Peperomia fagerlindii, P. prostrata, P. graveolens, P. hoffmannii, P. quadrangularis, Pilea depressa, Plectranthus prostratus

---

← TOP: This *Peperomia rubella* is at home in a 2-inch (5 cm) pot. BOTTOM, LEFT: Many *Peperomia* species are suited to growing both under glass and in the open on your windowsill. *Peperomia* sp. 'Baños, Ecuador', *P. prostrata, P. quadrangularis, P. rubella*. MIDDLE: *Peperomia quadrangularis* grows happily in a 1-inch (2.5 cm) ceramic pot. RIGHT: This is *Peperomia prostrata* growing in a 1-inch (2.5 cm) ceramic pot.

STRING OF PEARLS

S tring of pearls is a classic houseplant favorite, and for good reason. The unique, pearl-shaped leaves of this adorable succulent create a dramatic specimen in a tall pot or small hanging basket. A member of the aster family, these plants also produce beautiful white, pompom-like flowers from which you can collect seed. Flowers have a light cinnamon fragrance. String of pearls grows naturally in rocky outcroppings in South Africa. In their native habitat, they grow as a groundcover that is partially shaded by surrounding vegetation and rocks.

Size The stems of string of pearls may grow up to 3 inches (8 cm) tall (typically flush to the soil surface) before spilling over the edge of the pot to trail up to 2 feet (0.6 m). The round leaves are each about the size of a green pea.

Care While most succulents need high light, string of pearls is accustomed to filtered sun and is shaded from hot sun in its natural habitat. Provide part shade conditions by placing in an east-facing or unobstructed north-facing window, similar to how you grow Haworthia.

The chubby succulent leaves of string of pearls are designed to store extra water and reduce transpiration (water loss through the leaves). Each little leaf also has a translucent "window" to absorb extra light. Use small, porous containers with good drainage, because these plants have a relatively small root system. Allow soil to dry completely between waterings, and never let plants sit in excess water with soggy soil. Not sure when to water? Wait until you see leaves just beginning to shrivel. You can also grow them in wide, shallow planters to better manage moisture and allow plants to grow along the soil surface.

PLANT TYPE · Terrestrial

SKILL LEVEL · Easy to intermediate

LIGHT · Medium to high, no afternoon sun

SOIL · Loose, well-draining

MOISTURE · Low to medium, dry between waterings

HUMIDITY · Low

TEMPERATURE · Warm, 68°F to 80°F (20°C to 27°C)

FERTILIZER · Monthly, fall through spring at quarter strength

SIZE · 3 inches (8 cm) tall, 2- to 3-inch (5 to 8 cm) containers

PROPAGATION · Seeds, stem cuttings, clump division

GROW THE SAME WAY *Fenestraria rhopalophylla, Senecio citriformis, S. haworthii, S. herreianus, S. scaposus, S. radicans*

← The flowers on this cute little string of pearls growing in a 2-inch (5 cm) terracotta planter have matured and dried, offering up viable seed. INSET: The teardrop shaped leaves of the *Senecio citriformis* give it its common name, string of tears. This one is growing in a 2-inch (5 cm) white terracotta pot.

Carnivorous

I have a penchant for petite carnivorous plants, especially those that are easy to keep on a windowsill or open grow shelf. It is always fun to watch these fascinating plants capture insects and produce the cutest, tiniest blooms and pitchers. Plus, carnivorous plants that can be kept out in the open are handy for capturing fungus gnats from other houseplants.

When looking for tiny carnivorous species that are suited to easy-care windowsill culture, seek out terrestrial species that do not require a dormancy period. The easiest tiny carnivorous plants to grow on a sunny south- or west-facing windowsill are sundews, *Drosera* spp., with the cutest being the pygmy sundews. Some smaller species of American pitcher plant, *Sarracenia* spp., enjoy a sunny windowsill, as do Venus fly trap, although the latter's dormancy requirement can trip up less experienced growers.

If you want to flex your plant parent muscles, venture into the compact Australian pitcher plants (*Cephalotus* spp.), which are ridiculously adorable, if a bit trickier to grow. They also require a winter dormancy.

Low-light windows facing north or even east will not be the best option for carnivorous plants, but you can support some tiny species, such as Mexican butterworts (*Pinguicula* spp.) and bladderworts (*Utricularia* spp.), in such locations. That said, I find bladderworts tend to bloom better indoors in a sunny spot or with supplemental light.

Carnivorous plants don't have their own section in Chapter 4: Tiny Plants Under Glass (page 120) because most plants in this category are better suited to windowsill culture. Closed terrariums create the equivalent of tropical growing conditions rather than the naturally temperate habitat of many carnivorous species. Non-tropical carnivorous plants often struggle in the high-humidity conditions created in an enclosed environment.

Advanced terrarium construction and environmental controls can manage their very intense lighting and regular venting needs, but I recommend sticking with the few species that can do well under glass. You can grow some of my favorite tiny carnivorous species, such as tropical butterworts and terrestrial and epiphytic species of bladderwort (*Utricularia*), successfully in a Wardian case, under a cloche, or planted into an open terrarium or bubble bowl. They may tolerate enclosed planted terrarium culture. Beyond that, look for carnivorous plants specifically labeled as tropical if you plan to keep your carnivorous plants under glass.

← Pygmy sundew *Drosera omissa* × *pulchella* in bloom with tiny pink flowers.

PYGMY SUNDEW

G et out your magnifying glass because you will need it to get a good look at these teeny-tiny bug eaters! Truly the cutest of all the carnivorous plants, pygmy sundews also happen to be the easiest of the sundews to grow. Sticky droplets covering the tiny rosettes mimic morning dew, tempting insects onto the deadly trap. *D. patens × occidentalis* ssp. *Occidentalis* is a naturally occurring hybrid (not a human-made cross) with beautiful red coloration and relatively large pink flowers. The fifty known species of pygmy sundew are found primarily in southern parts of Western Australia. Unfortunately, this beautiful hybrid is extinct in the wild.

Size Most pygmy sundew grow to be less than 1 inch (less than 2.5 cm) wide, with variation. *D. patens × occidentalis* subsp. *occidentalis* typically grow to only ½ inch (1.3 cm). Surprisingly, plants have relatively long tap roots that can grow almost 8 inches (20 cm) long!

Care Pygmy sundews require high light or a full sun location. A bright southern or western exposure is best, or grow them directly under high-output LEDs. With high light, plants will develop more red color and flowers. Pygmy sundews prefer cool temperatures and actively grow winter through spring. While they do not require dormancy, hot temperatures can trigger it.

Always keep the pots of pygmy sundews sitting in a tray with 2 inches (5 cm) of rainwater or purified water. Refill the water tray when water is low. Cover plants with a cloche if you will be away from home for a week or more. Use pots 4 to 6 inches (10 to 15 cm) tall and wide to accommodate the long taproots. Plastic or sealed ceramic pots help retain moisture. Use a sandy carnivorous plant mix, and spray plants with a quarter-strength organic foliar feed monthly fall through spring.

PLANT TYPE · Terrestrial, bog

SKILL LEVEL · Easy to intermediate

LIGHT · High, full direct sun

SOIL · Well-draining sand/peat/coir mix, acidic

MOISTURE · Always wet; rainwater or purified water only

HUMIDITY · Not picky

TEMPERATURE · Cool to warm, 40°F to 80°F (5°C to 27°C)

FERTILIZER · Not required; if applied, use only foliar feed at quarter strength

SIZE · ½ inch (1.3 cm)

PROPAGATION · Gemmae, leaf-petiole cutting (stipule intact), seed (difficult)

GROW THE SAME WAY
Drosera dichrosepala, D. echinoblastus, D. mannii, D. micrantha, D. occidentalis, D. nitidula, D. omissa × pulchella, D. paleacea, D. scorpioides

← This colony of *Drosera patens × occidentalis* pygmy sundew is in flower.

MINIATURE TROPICAL (MEXICAN) BUTTERWORT

These delicate and sometimes translucent-looking carnivorous plants might seem intimidating to beginner plant parents, but tropical butterworts are relatively easy windowsill plants. While there are many species, I think *Pinguicula cyclosecta* is one of the prettiest. Plants produce flat rosettes of lavender to purple leaves, and can produce stunning metallic purple flowers. In summer months, plants catch insects on their sticky leaves. Tropical butterworts are found as lithophytes in fog forests in Central America and the Caribbean; native climates are warm, wet summers and cool, dry winters.

Size Miniature tropical butterworts rarely grow larger than 1 inch or so (3 cm) wide, with foliage that reaches only about ½ inch (1 cm) above the soil. Flower stems can reach 2 to 3 inches (5 to 8 cm) tall.

Care Plants need medium to high light or the equivalent of part sun conditions. Light requirements are slightly lower than for pygmy sundews, as butterworts often grow partially shaded in their natural habitat. An east-facing windowsill with morning sun is a good choice. In more light, the leaves of *P. cyclosecta* turn a lavender color that is quite lovely. You can also grow under LED grow lights.

No dormancy is required, but water needs vary seasonally. Keep plant pots sitting in about 1 inch (2.5 cm) of rainwater or purified water during summer when plants are growing and producing carnivorous leaves. During shorter winter days, when plants produce smaller succulent leaves, allow the water reservoir, and the soil, to dry before you refill.

Plants should be grown in a loose, rocky potting mix heavy on sand, perlite, or pumice. As with pygmy sundews, the roots are long, so use containers that are relatively tall and wide in comparison to the plant. Butterworts will also do well directly planted into open terrariums and even teacups. If fertilization is needed, spray plants with a quarter-strength organic foliar feed only when plants are producing carnivorous (sticky) leaves.

PLANT TYPE · Lithophyte, chasmophyte

SKILL LEVEL · Easy to intermediate

LIGHT · Medium to high, part sun

SOIL · Loose, rocky, slightly alkaline

MOISTURE · Rainwater or purified water; moist in summer, dry slightly in winter

HUMIDITY · Medium to high

TEMPERATURE · 50°F to 90°F (10°C to 32°C)

FERTILIZER · Not required; if applied, use only foliar feed at quarter-strength

SIZE · 1 inch (2.5 cm) wide

PROPAGATION · Seed, division

GROW THE SAME WAY *Pinguicula crassifolia, P. ehlersiae, P. emarginata, P. laueana, P. moranensis, P. rectifolia, Pinguicula* hybrids, *Cephalotus follicularis*

← *Pinguicula cyclosecta* usually sits in about 1 inch (2.5 cm) of rainwater.

love this teeny-tiny perennial terrestrial bladderwort, which quickly produces a dense carpet of itty-bitty leaves. As a bonus, bladderwort plants produce a profusion of flower stalks sporadically year-round, each sporting five to six individual white to pale violet blooms. It is a dramatic showing for such a tiny plant. *Utricularia livida* grows subterranean stolons that form the tiny leaves on top of the soil. The tiny bladder traps form underneath the soil and catch equally tiny creatures, such as fungus gnat larvae and nematodes. Bladderworts are the largest genus of carnivorous plants and are native to the tropical and sub-tropical regions of Mexico and South Africa. Currently, scientists have identified approximately 233 species.

Size The ¼-inch (0.6 cm) foliage of bladderwort grows flush with the soil surface, so it has the tiniest of profiles. Flower stalks reach 2 to 3 inches (5 to 7.5 cm) tall. Plant roots and underground bladder traps typically grow about 2 inches (5 cm) deep.

Care Bladderwort grows and blooms best with high light that mimics full sun exposure, so skip the north-facing window for a south- or west-facing one. Or, grow with high-light succulents under grow lights. You can even set this species outside on a sunny patio or balcony to grow outdoors spring through fall.

Plants do best in a sandy peat or coir potting mixture or chopped sphagnum moss mix that stays consistently moist. Heavily soak bladderwort four to five times per week, even daily if plants are in a tiny container. You can also mist them. You can grow plants in containers with a drainage hole and tray or in a watertight vessel with no drainage hole. If growing in a container with drainage holes, consider packing the bottom ½ inch (1.3 cm) of the pot with damp sphagnum moss to help maintain moisture, or always set the pot in about 1 inch (2.5 cm) of rainwater or distilled water. You do not need to grow *Utricularia livida* under glass or in a terrarium or aquarium, but they will do nicely in those conditions.

PLANT TYPE · Terrestrial, lithophyte

SKILL LEVEL · Easy

LIGHT · High, full sun

SOIL · Sandy coir mixture or sand/coir/sphagnum moss mixture

MOISTURE · Consistently moist; rainwater or purified water only

HUMIDITY · Medium

TEMPERATURE · Warm, 68°F to 80°F (20°C to 27° C), no dormancy

FERTILIZER · Not required; if applied, use only foliar feed at quarter-strength

SIZE · Leaves flush with soil, flower stems 2 to 3 inches (5 to 8 cm) tall

PROPAGATION · Division, seed

GROW THE SAME WAY
Utricularia sandersonii, U. subulata, U. pubescens

← Bladderwort, *Utricularia livida* 'Merrie Heart', is tiny enough to grow in a teacup. Moss helps retain moisture. INSET: Tiny underground bladder traps capture microscopic creatures.

Semi-Aquatic

Most semi-aquatic plants are best grown under glass, in paludariums or aquariums. However, I can recommend a handful of tiny semi-aquatics to grow without cover—as long as the plant's root system has constant access to water. When exploring the world of aquatic plants for windowsill culture, look for those native to areas that fluctuate seasonally between wet and drier times of year or plants that grow as groundcovers in marsh-like conditions. These species are better able to tolerate lower humidity.

← Tiny flowers emerge from my marsh pennywort.

MARSH PENNYWORT

*H*ydrocotyle sibthorpioides is quite versatile in its tolerance for a variety of growing conditions. This little gem has a mounding and running growth habit with bright green clover-like leaves. If you have ever grown a large Swedish ivy basket, marsh pennywort looks just like a miniature version! When grown as a potted plant with enough sunlight, plants will also produce tiny flowers. Marsh pennywort is a creeping plant native to tropical regions in Asia and Africa; however, it has been introduced and grows in many warm climates across the world. This species grows both as a creeping terrestrial plant as well as emersed in bodies of fresh water. Take note that it is invasive when introduced to bog or river areas and can also be a lawn "weed."

Size Plants grow to only about 1 inch (2.5 cm) tall, but the trailing stems can grow 1 foot (30 cm) or more in length. Plant leaves typically range from ¼ to ½ inches (0.6 to 1.3 cm) wide.

Care Plants need medium to high light or full sun conditions to look their best. Place them in a southern window exposure with plenty of bright light. Plants can also handle direct sun in an east- or west-facing window. I grow mine under supplemental LED lighting in a north-facing window. Plants growing in a terrarium will need bright supplemental light.

Provide plants constant access to water at their root zone, be it in wet soils potted or planted directly into an open terrarium. You can also grow plants aquatically in a paludarium or riparium. As a windowsill plant, pot marsh pennywort into a container with a drainage hole and always keep it submerged in 1 to 2 inches (2.5 to 5 cm) of water. If the pot is always sitting in water, you do not need to grow plants under glass. If plants run out of water at the root zone, foliage will quickly wilt. If you struggle to keep plants watered, place them under a cloche or inside a glass case to increase humidity.

PLANT TYPE • Terrestrial, aquatic

SKILL LEVEL • Easy

LIGHT • Medium to high, sun

SOIL • Heavier, moisture retentive

MOISTURE • Always wet, use water reservoir

HUMIDITY • Medium to high

TEMPERATURE • Cool to warm, 68°F to 80°F (20°C to 27°C)

FERTILIZER • Monthly at quarter strength

SIZE • 1 inch (2.5 cm) tall, stems trail to 12 inches (30 cm)

PROPAGATION • Stem cuttings, clump division

GROW THE SAME WAY
*Hydrocotyle tripartita,
Lindernia grandiflora,
Nertera depressa*

← Marsh pennywort (*Hydrocotyle sibthorpiodes*) grows quickly to form a tiny trailing windowsill plant.

4

tiny plants under glass

MANY TINY PLANTS, especially epiphytes, need higher relative humidity or wetter root zones than a typical open home environment provides. If you love high-humidity plants but simply cannot manage indoor humidity needs for large tropicals, then tiny plants are the way to go.

Place the high-humidity plants featured in this chapter under cloches, in glass canisters, Wardian cases, or other similar enclosed vessels. You can pot terrestrial species into planters and place them under glass or plant them directly into small terrariums and aquariums. Set epiphytes either on top of moist sphagnum moss inside glass jars or terrariums or mount them onto branches or tree fern bark. There are many ways to grow and display your gardens under glass.

While planted terrariums are popular, they can be more complicated to manage and move around. High-humidity plants that still need good root aeration may rot when planted in them. While I love building more complex terrariums and vivariums, I keep most of my tiny potted or mounted plant specimens set inside individual glass vessels or placed under cloches. Or, I use an orchidarium with a circulation fan. I can better appreciate and manage each plant specimen when grown individually. Doing so allows me to set these plants in windowsills or smaller spaces and have the flexibility to move them around my home for display.

Be sure to explore the "Grow the Same Way" sections for suggestions of many more tiny plants you can collect and grow under relatively similar conditions.

Foliage

While big aroids and other tropical foliage plants have captured the fancy of many plant parents these days, there is something exciting about finding teeny tiny versions of your favorite philodendron or fern. Once you delve into vendors who grow plants for aquariums and vivariums, you'll discover an entirely new world of miniature foliage.

Most foliage houseplants appreciate humidity on the higher side. These tiny tropicals require more humidity and moisture than a standard home can offer and so should be kept under glass—either in sealed jars or under a cloche—in a Wardian case or an orchidarium or planted in a terrarium or aquarium.

← My tiny *Pleopeltus percussa* fern in a glass jar.

Begonia 'Peridot' is a perky miniature rhizomatous Rex begonia well-suited for growing under glass or planting in a terrarium. Plants have silver-grey leaves with vibrant red stems. As plants age, they may exhibit different colors or characteristics, as is common with other rex begonias. The leaves of 'Peridot' may turn completely silver as they age or may turn a darker red or copper color. *Begonia rex-cultorum*, referred to as Rex begonias, is a group of cultivated hybrids begonias. All Rex begonia hybrids have as one parent the wild species *B. rex*, a native to rocky forests in Vietnam, southern China, northeastern India.

Size Leaves of 'Peridot' typically stay under 1½ inches (4 cm) in diameter. Plant height and width vary but are usually less than 8 inches (20 cm) tall and 2 to 3 inches (5 to 8 cm) wide.

Care Like most Rex begonias, 'Peridot' can tolerate variation in light exposure, from medium to high *indirect* light; always avoid hot, direct sunlight. Choose an east-facing exposure or a southern exposure set back from the window. You can also grow plants under grow lights.

'Peridot' needs consistent moisture and good aeration around its fine roots, and this can be a tricky combination. Always plant Rex begonias in porous clay pots with drainage holes to allow air and moisture to be exchanged at the root zone and reduce soggy conditions. Rotting or "melting"—which can happen in soggy conditions—means begonias need better air circulation. If this is an issue, set or plant your mini begonias in an open glass bubble bowl or use a vented cloche cover. I set potted specimens inside glass canisters, under a cloche, or in a Wardian case to increase surrounding humidity.

PLANT TYPE · Terrestrial

SKILL LEVEL · Intermediate

LIGHT · Medium to bright indirect light; no direct sun

SOIL · Loose, well-draining, mixed with chopped sphagnum moss

MOISTURE · Frequent watering, consistently moist; can tolerate some drying

HUMIDITY · Medium to high

TEMPERATURE · Cool to warm, 68°F to 80°F (20°C to 27°C)

FERTILIZER · Monthly at quarter strength

SIZE · 4 to 8 inches (10 to 20 cm) tall

PROPAGATION · Stem cuttings, leaf-petiole cuttings, split-vein cuttings, seed (challenging)

GROW THE SAME WAY
Begonia aridicaulis, B. dodsonii, B. geminiflora, B. minutifolia, B. rajah, B. 'Small Change', B. 'Maldonado', Gobenia vining begonias, such as B. segregata, B. tropaeolifolia, Peperomia turboensis

← This begonia 'Peridot' grows in a 2-inch (5 cm) pot.

MINIATURE OAKLEAF FIG

f you are familiar with miniature oakleaf fig's cousin *Ficus pumila* (creeping fig), you might think I am crazy for including this species. Creeping fig gets huge! Miniature oakleaf fig, on the other hand, stays much tinier, and sports what I think look like adorable tiny maple tree leaves. It is a slower grower than creeping fig and a perfect creeper for terrariums and vivariums. These species are native to tropical areas of South China through Malaysia.

Size The leaves of miniature oakleaf fig reach only ¼ to ½ inch (0.6 to 1.25 cm). Plants stay under 1 inch (2.5 cm) tall from soil level, with the vines reaching about 8 inches (20 cm) long.

Care Miniature oakleaf fig does very well in low light conditions, either on a north- or obstructed east-facing windowsill or with supplemental light from a low-intensity spotlight grow light. Mine lives happily in a glass jar in an east-facing windowsill that is totally shaded by a large evergreen oak tree. Plants do equally well grown under low-intensity grow lights or planted in low- to medium-light terrariums.

As is the case for most tropical vines, miniature oakleaf fig needs high relative humidity and consistently moist soil. Plants will attach and ramble over branches or tree fern backing in a terrarium. Its vining, rambling growth habit makes it perfect for hanging planters, but you may struggle to keep this plant hydrated indoors unless you grow it under glass. You can also train it to attach to and cover branches, driftwood, rocks, or other supports in a glass vessel or terrarium. If foliage becomes pale or chlorotic, mist with a liquid foliar feed or water in with a liquid feed monthly at quarter strength.

PLANT TYPE · Terrestrial vine, hemiepiphyte

SKILL LEVEL · Easy

LIGHT · Low, no direct sun

SOIL · Loose, well-draining

MOISTURE · Frequent watering, consistent moisture

HUMIDITY · High; terrarium planter, Wardian case, glass jar, or cloche

TEMPERATURE · Warm, 68°F to 80°F (20°C to 27°C)

FERTILIZER · Monthly at quarter to half strength

SIZE · 1 inch (2.5 cm) tall, 8 inch (20 cm) spread

PROPAGATION · Stem cuttings, division

GROW THE SAME WAY
Ficus pumilla varieties, *F. villosa*, *F. radicans*, *Marcgravia umbellata*, *M. rectiflora*, *Rhaphidophora cryptantha*, *R. pachyphylla*, *Pellionia* spp.

← Miniature oakleaf fig is a lovely, dainty little vine that loves high humidity. I keep this plant set inside a glass jar.

Clinging snake fern, or vine fern, is a charming miniature fern that is one of the easiest high-humidity ferns to grow for beginners. Plants have beautiful small, dark green fronds (leaves) that sit upright on the stems and have highly contrasted veins. This species also has the typical pubescent rhizome characteristic of many hemiepiphytic ferns. Native to the Caribbean and southern parts of Florida in the U.S., snake ferns are typically found growing as epiphytes. They can also be found growing as lithophytes.

Size The fronds of clinging snake fern are small, ranging in size from only ½ to ¾ inch (1.3 to 2 cm) in length. Plants kept in small pots will remain in petite clumps. Insert a stake or branch and vines will latch on and take off.

Care Like many ferns, clinging snake vine thrives in medium light conditions, shade, or part-shade, with no direct sunlight. Place in a north- or east-facing window or grow under low-intensity grow lights.

Plants are forgiving of both extremely wet and intermittently dry root zone conditions, which is why they are easy for beginners to grow, as long as plants are in a medium to high level of relative humidity. You can grow these plants in small, 2- to 3-inch (5 to 8 cm) pots and set inside glass vessels or cases. Plant directly into a terrarium or garden bowl in a well-draining terrarium mix or chopped sphagnum moss. Plants spread slowly to form a mat. Feed plants once per month with a liquid fertilizer or foliar feed at quarter strength.

PLANT TYPE · Hemiepiphyte

SKILL LEVEL · Easy

LIGHT · Low to medium light; no direct sun

SOIL · Loose, well-draining or chopped sphagnum moss

MOISTURE · Frequent watering, consistently moist but never soggy; tolerates some drying

HUMIDITY · High

TEMPERATURE · Warm, 68°F to 80°F (20°C to 27°C)

FERTILIZER · Monthly at quarter to half strength

SIZE · 1 inch (2.5 cm), length varies

PROPAGATION · Rhizome cuttings, division, spores (challenging)

GROW THE SAME WAY
Microgramma lycopoides, Lemmaphyllum microphyllum, Pyrrosia lanceolata, Pleopeltus percussa, Adiantum mariesii, Crepidomanes minutum, Asplenium holophlebium, Nephrolepis exaltata 'Suzi Wong'

← Clinging snake fern will happily reside long term in tiny, 2-inch (5 cm) containers placed under glass.

W hile you are probably familiar with the larger-leafed peperomia species, you may not have been introduced to the tiniest of micro peperomias. So tiny, in fact, that you must get up close or use a magnifying glass to fully appreciate their beautiful foliage patterns. This perky little peperomia is one of my favorite species for growing under glass in tiny containers. It is also a vivarium favorite. The tiny, nearly round leaves vary from deep to light green in color with striking red to burgundy between the veins. Stems can also turn a pinkish-red. While the species is not confirmed for this variety, it was discovered growing native around Baños de Agua Santa in Ecuador, a small sub-tropical highland-climate town located on an active volcano, that I had the pleasure to visit.

Size The beautiful tiny leaves reach only ¼ inch (0.6 cm). New leaves may emerge only ⅛ inch (0.3 cm) long. The delicate vines typically reach about 12 inches (30 cm) long.

Care Plants grow well in low to medium light conditions, shade, or part shade. This species can thrive in high *indirect* light conditions. If leaves begin to fade or bleach, they are getting too much light or too much direct sun. You can grow these plants in standard pots, but stems will also vine and produce aerial roots that will attach to nearby substrate or moss. Always keep the root zone of the plant moist. This tiny peperomia is both slow to root and produce new shoots. If you leave plants or cuttings uncovered or in open-air containers, they will quickly shrivel up. You may be able to transition a mature, established plant to an open-air environment, but only with regular misting.

PLANT TYPE · Hemiepiphyte

SKILL LEVEL · Intermediate

LIGHT · Low to medium, no direct sun

SOIL · Loose, well-draining

MOISTURE · Consistently moist, not soggy

HUMIDITY · Medium to high

TEMPERATURE · Cool to warm, 68°F to 80°F (20°C to 27°C)

FERTILIZER · Foliar feed monthly at quarter strength

SIZE · ½ inch tall (1.25 cm), vine length varies

PROPAGATION · Stem cuttings, division

GROW THE SAME WAY
Marcgravia spp., *Peperomia antoniana*, *P. emarginella*, *P. eburnea*, *P. fagerlindii*, *P. guttulata*, *P. velutina*, *P. villacaulus*, *Peperomia* 'Silver Stripe', *Pilea depressa*

← *Peperomia* sp. 'Baños, Ecuador' grows happily under glass or in terrariums.

MINIATURE PHILODENDRON

have never seen a tinier variety of philodendron than 'Mini Santiago'! Several rare miniature philodendron species have entered the plant market from places such as Ecuador and Peru in recent years, but their nomenclature is still evolving. Such is the case for this species. 'Mini Santiago' is a tiny vining philodendron sporting petite, bright emerald-green leaves with beautiful and sculptural deep veining texture. Très chic! It was discovered growing as a hemiepiphytic vine near the town of Santiago in subtropical Ecuador.

Size The tiny leaves of 'Mini Santiago' grow to less than 1 inch (2.5 cm) long and about ½ inch (1.25 cm) wide. While I am not certain of a maximum length of the vines, plants are very slow-growing and it is doubtful you will ever need much space for this tiny aroid.

Care 'Mini Santiago' grows well in low to medium, indirect light: a north-facing exposure or low-intensity grow lighting 2 feet (61 cm) above the plants is adequate. If you are growing in a terrarium with artificial light, make sure plants are not too close to the light source. If foliage is a bright emerald green and not curled, then light is ideal; leaves will curl and become pale green to yellow if light volume is too high. Internode length will also decrease at high light levels.

Keep plants consistently moist with high relative humidity under a glass cloche, canister, or Wardian case or planted in a terrarium or vivarium. When humidity is adequate, long, furry white aerial roots emerge from the stem nodes. If plants have something to attach to or contact the growing media or moss, the aerial roots will latch on or root in. You can grow 'Mini Santiago' to cover mossed branches or porous supports. Plants can be slow and finicky to root and grow, so patience is required. Mist with a foliar feed at quarter strength monthly.

PLANT TYPE · Hemiepiphyte

SKILL LEVEL · Intermediate

LIGHT · Low to medium indirect light; no direct sun

SOIL · Loose, well-draining

MOISTURE · Frequent watering, consistent moisture

HUMIDITY · Medium to high

TEMPERATURE · Cool to warm, 60°F to 80°F (16°C to 27°C)

FERTILIZER · Foliar feed monthly at quarter strength

SIZE · 1 inch (2.5 cm), vine length varies

PROPAGATION · Stem cuttings with node or aerial root; slow to root

GROW THE SAME WAY *Philodendron pteromischum*, *P.* 'Tingo Maria Mini', *P.* sp. 'Condor', *P.* sp. 'Mini Ecuador'

← A rooted cutting of *Philodendron* 'Mini Santiago' is comfortable in a tiny, 1½-inch (4 cm) ceramic planter.

SPIKEMOSS OR CLUBMOSS

f you love moss and ferns, you will undoubtedly fall in love with tiny spikemoss. Species of *Selaginella* look like a cross between the two but are in fact neither a moss nor a fern. They are lycopods! Spikemosses are prehistoric fern relatives (also called fern allies) and are vascular plants that do produce spores. *Salaginella kraussiana* var. *brownii* is one of my favorite varieties, due to its perfectly lush, mound-like habit and cheery chartreuse foliage. The bright feathery foliage brightens up any glass jar, bubble bowl, or terrarium planting. Most species of *Selaginella* are native to tropical regions of South America, South, Africa, and Australia. *S. kraussiana* is native to mild, wet, and cloudy regions of Africa and the Azores.

Size *S. kraussiana* var. *brownii* is particularly petite, growing to only about 1 inch (2.5 cm) tall and perhaps 2 to 3 inches (5 to 8 cm) wide. The tiny lanceolate leaves grow to only $1/100$ to $7/50$ inch (2.5 to 3.6 mm) by $3/100$ to $1/20$ inch (0.8 to 1.2 mm).

Care *S. kraussiana* var. *brownii* is one of the easiest spikemoss species to grow, especially in tiny spaces. Plants are happy growing in low-light conditions, such as a north-facing window. However, plants may grow a bit more vigorously in an east-facing window or with a few hours of supplemental grow lighting. Avoid direct sunlight as it can burn plants.

  Salaginella need constant moisture and high humidity, with good root aeration. Do not let them dry out. Make sure to use a loose, well-draining potting mix if planting in containers, or a loose terrarium mix if planting in such an enclosure. Set plants inside glass canisters, under cloches, or plant directly into a terrarium. These are also favorite choices for vivarium plantings. My potted specimens grow happily in small, closed glass jars, where I rarely need to provide any extra water. Spray with a foliar feed bi-monthly at quarter strength.

PLANT TYPE · Terrestrial

SKILL LEVEL · Easy

LIGHT · Low light, no direct sun

SOIL · Loose, well-draining

MOISTURE · Frequent watering, constant moisture

HUMIDITY · Medium to high

TEMPERATURE · Warm, 68°F to 80°F (20°C to 27°C)

FERTILIZER · 4 to 6 times per year at quarter to half strength

SIZE · 1 to 2 inches (2.5 to 5 cm)

PROPAGATION · Division, stem cutting, spores

GROW THE SAME WAY
*Selaginella erythropus,
S. emmeliana, S. uncinata,
S. moellendorffii, S. rupestris*

← My *Selaginella* grows in a 2-inch (5 cm) pot, which sits inside a glass jar.

BABY'S TEARS

Baby's tears is one of the most delicate-looking tiny plants you can grow. But this diminutive member of the nettle family, and Pilea relative, can be quite the assertive grower in the right environment. Because of its tiny round leaves and dense matted growth habit, from a distance you might confuse this tiny spreader for moss. Plants will spread out over the soil in a terrarium or trail over the edges of a pot. The species is a medium bright green color, but there is also a lovely yellow-green variety called 'Aurea'. Baby's tears, along with other nettles, is native to the Mediterranean climates of southern Europe, specifically Sardinia and Corsica.

Size The tiny leaves of baby's tears typically grow to less than ¼ inch (0.6 cm). Plants grow in trailing mounds with the upward growth typically only reaching about 2 inches (5 cm) tall. Trailing stems can reach up to 12 inches (30 cm) long.

Care Plants will thrive in low light with no direct sun; however, if plants seem weak in a north-facing exposure move them to an eastern exposure or provide a few hours of supplemental light from low-intensity grow lights. You will often see baby's tears touted as an easy windowsill houseplant; it is also used as an outdoor groundcover or container plant in the right climates. However, I find as a houseplant it dries out far too quickly to be left on an open windowsill. I always grow mine under glass or planted into terrariums. Keep the root zone moist but make sure pots have good drainage. If you want to grow baby's tears out in the open, try growing it like *Hydrocotyle* (page 118).

PLANT TYPE · Terrestrial

SKILL LEVEL · Easy to intermediate

LIGHT · Low to medium, part shade; no direct sun

SOIL · Loose, well-draining

MOISTURE · Frequent watering, consistently moist

HUMIDITY · Medium to high

TEMPERATURE · Cool to warm, 50°F to 80°F (10°C to 27°C)

FERTILIZER · Monthly at quarter strength

SIZE · 2 to 4 inches (5 to 10 cm) tall, trailing to 12 inches (30 cm)

PROPAGATION · Stem cuttings, division

GROW THE SAME WAY
Pilea microphylla 'Variegata'

← *Soleirolia soleirolii* 'Aurea' grows in a 1½- inch (4 cm) pot that I keep in a glass jar.

Flowering

Many types of plants grown for their flowers do best in high humidity. Quite a few of the micro-mini flowering plants are epiphytes, falling into the micro orchid category. For best success, I typically keep my high-humidity micro orchids in a Wardian case or glass canister. For high-humidity species that need better air circulation, I use an orchidarium with a fan or a cloche with a vent hole.

If you prefer to stick to potted plants, there are plenty of terrestrial bloomers for growing under glass, especially in the gesneriad and begonia groups. While many gesneriads and begonias can fare well in open windowsill culture, some need the higher-humidity environment created by growing under glass.

The tiniest bloomers I include here are in the genus *Sinningia*, often erroneously referred to as miniature Gloxinia. Fair warning: it has been years since micro sinningia had their heyday (we are talking the 1960s and '70s, the last big houseplant craze wave). Finding these tiny gems is not always easy, but I am on a mission to revive their popularity. You may have the best luck finding seed of *S. pusilla*, while plants of some of the hybrid cultivars may be more available in limited quantities. There is typically slightly better availability on larger miniature and standard sinningia. As far as I am concerned, plant hunting for a rare and worthy species is time well spent.

Deadheading—removing spent flowers—is an important task when you keep blooming plants under glass in humid conditions. When flowers senesce and fall, they decay and can breed mildew or other fungal decay pathogens that will damage plants, especially if they fall on plant foliage. Always keep old, spent flowers snipped off your terrarium bloomers to help keep the growing environment clean.

← *Sinningia* 'Freckles', a miniature hybrid cultivar.

DWARF BEGONIA

Begonia prismatocarpa is often touted as the smallest of all begonias, although I think *B. vankerckhovenii* gives it a run for its money. One of the few yellow flowering begonias, *B. prismatocarpa* has shimmery light green fuzzy leaves and produces a continuous abundance of cute, round yellow to yellow-orange blooms. It grows as an epiphyte or lithophyte with trailing stems, making it a natural for mounting in terrariums or orchidariums. However, plants can also handle being grown in open terrariums and bubble bowls in a brightly lit office or apartment. *B. prismatocarpa* is native to tropical Western Africa and was first discovered on the Equatorial Guinean island of Bioko.

Size Leaves of these little cuties are about ½ to 1 inch (1.3 to 2.5 cm) long, and plants reach only 3 to 4 inches (8 to 10 cm) tall. Clumps spread via its semi-vining stems and creeping rhizomes.

Care *B. prismatocarpa* needs medium to high light to stay in bloom regularly. Choose an east-facing exposure, or a southern exposure with protection from direct sun. Grow on light shelves 12 to 14 inches (30 to 36 cm) below the light source (or a grow lamp in a terrarium/aquarium). If plants are growing lots of foliage but no flowers, increase the light volume or duration.

Plants need consistent moisture at their root zone and medium to high humidity. Soggy soil can quickly rot or melt plants. Avoid leaving water on the leaves; instead water at the root zone. Mount as an epiphyte or grow in small pots using a loose gesneriad potting mix. While plants do need high humidity and won't always tolerate open windowsill culture, you can get away with planting *B. prismatocarpa* in vented bubble bowls or under a vented cloche, where humidity will still be higher than normal in your home. Fertilize monthly with a liquid feed at quarter strength, at the root zone.

PLANT TYPE · Terrestrial, epiphyte, lithophyte

SKILL LEVEL · Intermediate

LIGHT · Medium to high

SOIL · Sphagnum moss/mounted on bark, gesneriad potting mix

MOISTURE · Consistently moist, rainwater

HUMIDITY · Medium to high

TEMPERATURE · Cool to warm, 70°F to 80°F (20°C to 27°C) day, 60°F to 62°F (16°C to 17°C) night

FERTILIZER · Monthly, spring and summer at quarter to half strength

SIZE · 3 to 4 inches (8 to 10 cm) tall

PROPAGATION · Whole-leaf cuttings, leaf-petiole cuttings, rhizome cuttings, seed

GROW THE SAME WAY
Begonia ficicola, B. lichenora, B. microsperma, B. staudtii, B. vittariifolia, B. × 'Buttercup'

← *B. prismatocarpa* sports tiny yet cheery yellow blooms.

DWARF BEGONIA

An adorable flowering specimen for growing under glass, this delicate micro-mini begonia sports cheery bright yellow flowers almost continuously. The teardrop-shaped leaves are bright to dark green with softly serrated red edges. The pale petioles are exceptionally long, giving this begonia a draping growth habit. This is a versatile begonia you can grow either potted or mounted onto moss or tree fern panels in a terrarium or orchidarium. It will even grow as a lithophyte if there is enough surrounding moss. Plants look similar to *B. prismatocarpa* but are usually smaller. *B. vankerckhovenii* grows native in the tropical regions of Zaire, West Africa.

Size One of the smallest of begonias, the leaves of *B. vankerckhovenii* reach only about 1 to 2 inches (2.5 to 5 cm) long. Depending on how you grow them, clumps can reach up to 7 inches (18 cm) tall but often fall over to cascade downward. You can keep this miniature in tiny, 1- to 3-inch (2.5 to 8 cm) pots.

Care Plants grow well in low to medium light levels in a north- or east-facing window or with low-intensity grow lamps. If using grow lights, keep them 18 to 24 inches (46 to 61 cm) above plants and avoid too much direct light. If plants are not blooming, increase the light volume or duration. Plants stay more compact in higher light.

    B. vankerckhovenii need constant high humidity and root zone moisture. That said, they do not appreciate water on the foliage, so only spray or water the roots. They are happiest growing in chopped sphagnum moss but also do well in loose gesneriad potting mix with drainage or mounted in terrariums or vivariums. When grown mounted, plants drape in a lovely cascading form. Clumps can spread via their rhizomes. Apply a liquid fertilizer to the root zone monthly at quarter strength to keep plants blooming.

PLANT TYPE • Terrestrial, epiphyte, lithophyte

SKILL LEVEL • Intermediate

LIGHT • Medium, shade to part shade

SOIL • Sphagnum moss/mounted on bark, gesneriad potting mix

MOISTURE • Consistent moisture, rainwater

HUMIDITY • Medium to high

TEMPERATURE • Cool grower, 70°F to 80°F (21°C to 27°C) day, 60°F to 62°F night (16 to 17°C)

FERTILIZER • Monthly, spring and summer at quarter to half strength

SIZE • Leaves 1 to 1½ inch (2.5 to 4 cm), flowers 2 to 3 inch (5 to 8 cm) tall

PROPAGATION • Whole-leaf cuttings, leaf-petiole cuttings, rhizome cuttings, seed

GROW THE SAME WAY *Begonia prismatocarpa, B. ficicola. B. lichenora, Triolena pileoides, Biophytum soukupii*

← I keep this *Begonia vankerckhovenii* planted in chopped moss in demi-tasse cup and under a cloche. This young specimen will eventually grow to fill up the tiny cup.

The flowers of the tiny icicle orchid are truly exquisite. As the purple-spotted flower petals unfurl, they reveal transparent, tear-shaped appendages that resemble dangling icicles. These dangling appendages are meant to attract pollinators, such as small flies. I usually jump up and down with joy when my specimen starts putting out flower buds from the 2-inch (5 cm) cluster of leaves. As a bonus, this species flowers sporadically throughout the year. Species of the genus *Stelis* (many previously placed in the genus *Pleurothallis*) are epiphytic orchids native to cool areas in Mexico, Guatemala, and El Salvador. There are about 500 known species in the genus *Stelis* alone, and thousands of Pleurothallids for you to discover.

Size Icicle orchids produce 1- to 1½-inch (2.5 to 4 cm) leaves and 2- to 3-inch (5 to 8 cm) inflorescences. The leaves and roots typically make a 2- to 3-inch (5 to 8 cm) clump.

Care Many micro orchids in the Pleurothallid group (also called leach orchids) are well-suited for orchid beginners. Medium light conditions are best, but plants tolerate lower light that would mimic shaded conditions outdoors. Higher light is fine if it is not direct sunlight.

House these little gems under a cloche, in a glass canister, an orchidarium, or mounted inside a terrarium. They do like good air movement, so I usually recommend placing in a glass vessel that has ventilation or a lid that can be removed or vented. Water the base of the plant/roots with rainwater or purified water several times per week, allowing plants to approach dryness before watering or misting again. If you can mist roots once or twice per day, try windowsill culture. Plants prefer cool temperatures.

PLANT TYPE · Epiphyte

SKILL LEVEL · Intermediate to advanced

LIGHT · Medium

SOIL · Sphagnum moss/mounted on bark

MOISTURE · Frequent watering, rainwater, almost dry between watering

HUMIDITY · Medium

TEMPERATURE · Cool grower; 70°F to 80°F (20°C to 27°C) day, 60°F to 62°F (16°C to 17°C) night

FERTILIZER · Monthly, spring and summer at quarter to half strength

SIZE · Leaves 1 to 1½ inches (2.5 to 4 cm), flowers 2 to 3 inches (5 to 8 cm) tall

PROPAGATION · Division

GROW THE SAME WAY *Stelis* spp., *Pleurothallis grobyi* (see more micro orchid recommendations on page 147)

← I mounted this icicle orchid with moss on a small piece of bark, and was rewarded with its fascinating blooms.

↑ A *Dracula* orchid shows off its tiny, happy blooms.

← Grown primarily for its beautiful foliage, a coveted *Lepanthes calodictyon* in bud and about to bloom; this species needs cool temperatures to thrive.

There are many micro orchids you can grow similarly to icicle orchid. Conditions may vary slightly, of course, between different species and varieties, but in general these are types you can keep and maintain similarly under glass. Many of these species will also tolerate open windowsill culture with extra humidity from daily (or twice daily) mistings or a nearby humidifier. Be sure to research the specific growing recommendations for each species and group together plants with similar needs. I encourage you to experiment and have fun!

HERE ARE A FEW ADDITIONAL MICRO ORCHIDS TO TRY:
Aerangis spp., *Angraecum* spp., *Barbosella orbicularis*, *Bulbophyllum* spp., *Cattleya* spp.
Dendrobium spp., *Dracula* spp., *Dryadella pusiola*, *D. zebrina*, *Erycina pusilla*,
Lepanthes spp., *Leptotes* spp., *Masdevallia bucculenta*, *Masdevallia* spp., *Pleurothallis* spp.,
Neofinetia falcala, *Ornithocephalus* spp., *Platystele* spp., *Promenaea* spp., *Sophronitis* spp.,
Specklinia spp., *Stelis* spp., *Tolumnia* spp.

← My icicle orchids may reside in glass canisters. I vent or remove the lid every couple of days for air circulation.

Sinningia pusilla

MICRO SINNINGIA

This is the queen, in my opinion, of the tiny blooming gesneriads. Part of what makes *Sinningia pusilla* so coveted is the large bloom size to plant ratio. Plants hardly seem big enough to support the flowers! *S. pusilla* plants grow in a rosette with oval, olive-green leaves and rusty red veins from a pinhead-sized, fleshy tuber. A profusion of tubular lavender flowers float on wire-thin stems about 1 inch (2.5 cm) above the foliage. The flowers can have creamy white to yellow throats, and plants bloom freely throughout the year. *S. pusilla*, along with three micro species (*S. concinna, S. muscicola,* and *S. minima*), all commonly cross-hybridized, are native to the state of Rio de Janeiro in Brazil.

Size *S. pusilla* grows up to only 1 inch (2.5 cm) tall. Mature plants grow and bloom happily in thimble-sized containers. No need to use a container any larger than 2 inches (5 cm) wide. Hybrid miniature sinningia grow a bit larger, reaching 2 to 4 inches (5 to 10 cm) tall.

Care Plants thrive in low to medium indirect light: north-facing windows or low-intensity grow lights are ideal. When grown on a grow light shelf, plants can sit to the edge, away from direct light. If plants don't bloom, increase light volume or duration.

Keep root systems consistently moist with rainwater or purified water. *S. pusilla* and other micro species and hybrids are best potted and kept under glass, set inside a jar, under a cloche, or inside a Wardian case to keep humidity high and soil consistently moist. Plant them directly into an enclosed terrarium or paludarium only if it has good drainage. The "larger" miniature species and hybrids do best with more air circulation—under a vented cloche or open terrarium that can be misted. Plants have a very tiny, loose root system; handle and deadhead with extreme care. If plants suddenly lose foliage, they may need a short dormancy. Reduce watering for a few weeks until you see new growth, then resume watering.

PLANT TYPE · Terrestrial

SKILL LEVEL · Intermediate to advanced

LIGHT · Low to medium

SOIL · Soilless gesneriad mix or sphagnum moss

MOISTURE · Frequent watering, rainwater or purified water, keep moist

HUMIDITY · Medium to high

TEMPERATURE · Warm, 68°F to 80°F (20°C to 27°C)

FERTILIZER · 6 times per year at quarter strength (easily burned)

SIZE · 1 inch (2.5 cm) tall and wide

PROPAGATION · Seeds, stem cuttings, division of tubers

GROW THE SAME WAY
Diastema spp., *Episcia* spp., *Sinningia concinna,*
S. minima, S. muscicola,
S. hirsuta

← TOP, LEFT: I keep this tiny colony of *Sinningia pusilla* 'Itaoca' growing and blooming in a 1½-inch (4 cm) ceramic planter inside a glass jar or under a cloche. TOP, RIGHT: A robust clump of *Sinningia* 'Mighty Mouse' grows in a true-to-size eggshell planter. BOTTOM, LEFT: Like this *Sinningia* 'Freckles', I keep most of my sinningia, and other high-humidity plant specimens, in glass jars for extra humidity. BOTTOM, RIGHT: I removed a few of my sinningia from under glass for display. Clockwise from top: Larger miniature hybrids S. × 'Flair', S. × 'Powderpuff', S. × 'Freckles', S. × 'HCY's Taurus'; and micro species S. *pusilla* 'Itaoca' and S. *pusilla*.

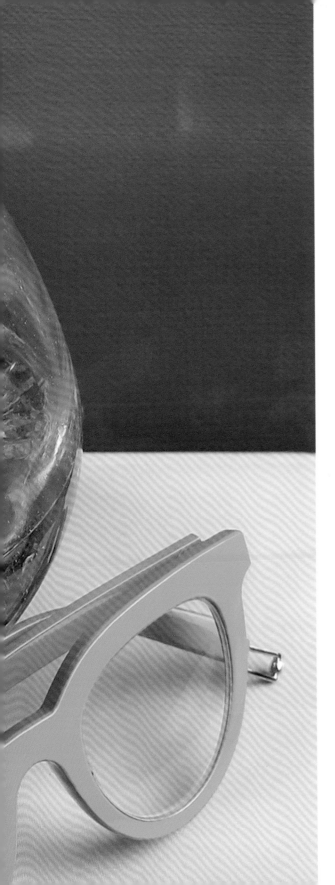

Aquatic & Semi-Aquatic

There are several tiny plants sold as submersible freshwater aquarium plants that also do quite well as floating specimens, grown in Leca and water, or mounted epiphytically in high-humidity ripariums, paludariums or terrariums. This category is where you will discover some tiny aroids that probably will be new to you.

I have highlighted a few of my favorite semi-aquatic and aquatic species you can grow fully submersed, emersed, floated, or mounted. Many of these species will do best under a glass cover or closed vessel to provide constant humidity, especially if mounted as an epiphyte. However, those growing fully submersed, floating, or emersed directly in water can thrive in vented vessels or tanks with open tops, if you maintain adequate water levels.

← Several *Anubias* grow on top of rocks in a bubble bowl alongside some floating crystalwort.

DWARF ANUBIAS

A*nubias barteri* var. *nana* 'Petite' is a lovely little philodendron relative primarily sold for aquarium culture, but it can be grown in several different ways. These undemanding aroids have a deep emerald-green color and a tight clumping growth habit. Once mature, plants will even offer up lovely little white spadix blooms on a ½- to 2-inch (1.3 to 5 cm) petiole. In fact, this species looks just like a teeny-tiny version of a peace lily, especially when in flower. Such sophistication on such a tiny scale. Anubias are native to Cameroon in West Africa, where they primarily grow in rivers, streams, and marshes.

Size A. 'Petite' lives up to its name, growing to only 1 inch (2.5 cm) tall. The tiny leaves reach about ⅗ inch (1.5 cm) and grow attached to a small rhizome. Plants are slow growing but given time, the tiny clumps can create a small green "carpet" when planted in a terrarium.

Care Plants thrive in low light or shade conditions. If leaves begin to grow pale or bleach, plants are getting too much direct light or sun. Choose north- or east-facing windows or low-intensity grow lights. If plants are not growing, slightly increase light volume.

You can grow Anubias completely submersed under water with bright aquarium lighting; but plants are happier growing emersed in water, with the rhizome and leaves just above the surface. Use Leca, pebbles, or crushed glass in a bowl or cup. Cover the container with a cloche if water evaporates too quickly. You can also mount plants on stones, driftwood, or bark and place them inside a glass canister or terrarium. If planting directly into a terrarium, never bury the horizontal-growing rhizome under potting soil or moss, which can cause plants to rot. Occasionally add some diluted liquid fertilizer to the water or mist with a diluted foliar feed.

PLANT TYPE · Aquatic, epiphyte, hemiepiphyte

SKILL LEVEL · Easy to intermediate

LIGHT · Low, shade

SUBSTRATE · Float or submerse in water, Leca; mounted on moss, bark, aquarium soil

MOISTURE · Constant; rainwater or purified water

HUMIDITY · Medium to high

TEMPERATURE · Cool to warm, 68°F to 82°F (20°C to 28°C)

FERTILIZER · 6 times per year at quarter to half strength

SIZE · 1 inch (5 cm) tall

PROPAGATION · Rhizome cutting

GROW THE SAME WAY *Anubias barteri* var. *nana* 'Petite White', 'Golden', 'Thick Leaf', and *Bucephalandra* spp., *Cryptocoryne parva*

← This dwarf anubias specimen grows in a small shot glass with pebbles and rainwater. INSET: This dwarf Anubias is small enough to grow in Leca and water in a teacup.

BABY LEAF BOLBITIS,
MINI AFRICAN WATER FERN

One of the tiniest and cutest ferns you can get your hands on, this variety of *Bolbitis* is a super-dwarf variety of its parent species. Its tiny, feathery fronds are also more deeply lobed, and are deep emerald green and quite elegant. Baby leaf bolbitis grows naturally in tropical West African regions from Ethiopia to Senegal, as well as in northern South Africa. Plants typically grow along the margins of waters with heavy currents, anchoring themselves to rocks and driftwood.

Size The fronds of baby leaf bolbitis typically grow to only 2 to 4 inches (5 to 10 cm) tall, with clumps growing 2 to 3 inches (5 to 8 cm) wide. The standard species grows to 6 to 16 inches (15 to 40 cm).

Care Plants do well when grown in low to medium light levels, such as a northern or eastern exposure. They also grow nicely under low-intensity grow lights or aquarium lighting, but make sure they are not placed too close to the light source.

While you can grow baby leaf bolbitis as a terrestrial potted plant, never bury the rhizomes under the soil or they will rot. You can also grow them completely submersed with bright grow lighting or in a paludarium or riparium. Like Anubias, they are happier growing emersed, with foliage and rhizome above water and the root system just below or touching water. If you grow it emersed out in the open, use Leca or aquaponic grow baskets (which I use in mason jars) and mist plants regularly. Mount plants to pieces of driftwood and keep them in a humid terrarium, glass canister, or paludarium. Plants are slow growers and fertilization is rarely needed, but you can add a diluted liquid fertilizer to the water several times per year.

PLANT TYPE · Aquatic, epiphyte, hemiepiphyte

SKILL LEVEL · Easy to intermediate

LIGHT · Low to medium

SUBSTRATE · Water and Leca, terrarium mix, rocks, bark, nutrient-rich terrarium potting mix

MOISTURE · Constant; rainwater or purified water

HUMIDITY · Medium to high

TEMPERATURE · Cool to warm, 65°F to 80°F (18°C to 26°C)

FERTILIZER · Not necessary; can apply 3 to 4 times per year at quarter strength

SIZE · 2 to 4 inches (5 to 10 cm) tall

PROPAGATION · Rhizome cutting, division

GROW THE SAME WAY
*Microsorum pteropus,
Trichomanes javanicum*

← Baby leaf *Bolbitis* is growing emersed in Leca and water in a small canning jar. INSET: Baby leaf *Bolbitis* can also grow mounted on driftwood set in rainwater in a glass canister.

FLOATING CRYSTALWORT

f you ever wanted to grow a liverwort, this tiny species is for you! Crystalwort, also called floating crystalwort, is a super easy and fast-growing spreader—extra friendly—that you can grow in a variety of fun ways. Plus, it is very pretty. These bright green bryophytes grow in an elongated finger- or threadlike form.

Crystalwort is native to many areas across Asia, Africa, and the Americas. Plants naturally grow as a floating species in ponds or calm streams.

Size Crystalwort typically grows in a threadlike fashion to about 1 inch (2.5 cm), but clumps quickly expand to create large mats. Trim plants or simply pull the clumps apart with your fingers to keep size under control or to divide.

Care Crystalwort thrives in varied light conditions. If plants are floating on the water's surface in an aquarium or other glass vessel, low light or shade is fine. Plants will turn pale yellow green in too much light. If you attach crystalwort to rocks or other features submerged in an aquarium or riparium, then increase to medium to high light. Plants will brown if they do not get enough light.

Crystalwort does not require any substrate to survive; it only needs to be surrounded by water all the time. Float plants in water in a teacup, bowl, or vase with water, or add it to a paludarium or ripairum. They will also attach nicely to any moist, porous surface, such as rocks, driftwood, or terracotta. I even use this species to cover water-wicking clay vessels on which I grow micro orchids and mosses. Add a little diluted natural fertilizer to the water monthly. This liverwort does not extract nutrients through a typical root system. Instead, it absorbs nutrients through its leaves and stems.

PLANT TYPE · Aquatic, freshwater

SKILL LEVEL · Easy

LIGHT · Low to medium, shade

SUBSTRATE · Rainwater, purified water, any consistently moist porous surface

MOISTURE · Constant; rainwater or purified water

HUMIDITY · Medium to high

TEMPERATURE · Cool to warm, 59°F to 86°F (15°C to 30°C)

FERTILIZER · Monthly at quarter strength added to water

SIZE · 1 inch (2.5 cm)

PROPAGATION · Pull apart clumps to divide

GROW THE SAME WAY
Nymphoides aquatica, Phyllanthus fluitans, Salvinia cucullata, S. natans, Taxiphyllum barbieri

← A cute little cluster of crystalwort floats in a teacup filled with some crushed glass and rainwater. See how it attaches to the surrounding surfaces. INSET: I often float crystalwort in a variety of glass vessels with other high-humidity plant companions, such as this potted *Selaginella*.

SPOTLESS WATERMEAL

have saved the tiniest plant for last. Species in the *Wolffia* genus, commonly known as water-meal or duckweed, are the tiniest known species of flowering vascular plants on earth! You need a microscope to see their miniscule flowers. While this is not a species commonly kept as a houseplant, I could not pass on including this incredible novelty, which can float in small glass vessels, aquariums, paludariums, and ripariums. Float it by itself or grow as a companion to other aquatic or semi-aquatic plants. Watermeal is the ultimate in minimalist botanical style and is a high-protein edible plant. Different species are found growing all over the world, including the tropics *and* Siberia.

Size *Wolffia arrhiza* has a tiny oval structure that is all of ¹⁄₅₀ to ¹⁄₂₀ inch (0.4 to 1.3 mm) long and ¹⁄₁₂₅ to ¹⁄₂₅ inch (0.2 to 1 mm) wide. *W. globosa* is slightly smaller and considered the tiniest of all flowering species.

Care

Watermeal can be overly easy . . . or incredibly frustrating to grow. You may fail with it several times before getting it right. Naturally floating just under the surface of still freshwater, it needs exposure to medium or high light or a sunny location. Use a tub, open glass vessel, or aquarium filled with fresh rainwater. Set it in a south-facing window, out on a balcony, or under high-output LEDs. Do not set it too close to grow lights, because plants prefer cool temperatures. If you use a vessel with a lid, vent it regularly.

Watermeal often grows best with other aquatic plant companions. If water quality is not ideal, plants may sink to the bottom and go into a dormancy. Fertilizer is not necessary, but you can add diluted natural liquid fertilizers to the water.

PLANT TYPE · Aquatic, freshwater

SKILL LEVEL · Intermediate to advanced

LIGHT · Medium to bright

MOISTURE · Constant, rainwater or purified water with a neutral to alkaline pH

HUMIDITY · Medium to high; pauladrium, aquarium, riparium, watertight glass vessel

TEMPERATURE · Cool to warm, 59°F to 86°F (15°C to 30°C)

FERTILIZER · Not necessary

SIZE · ¹⁄₁₂₅ to ¹⁄₂₀ inch (0.2 to 1.3 mm)

PROPAGATION · Plants multiply vegetatively; separate clumps into new container

GROW THE SAME WAY
Wolffia spp., *Lemmna* spp., *Sprirodela* spp., *Landoltia* spp., *Wolffiella* spp.

Never release aquatic plants into the outdoors, ponds, or local waterways. They may be non-native to your region and/or invasive. Invasive plants can wreak havoc on local ecosystems.

← Duckweed grows floating in a tiny glass jar. This species is edible and can be cultivated for human consumption (and your aquarium dwellers will love it too!).

5

displaying tiny plants

TINY PLANTS afford you a lot of flexibility—and creativity—with your indoor gardening activities and décor. Once you have built up a small or sizeable tiny plant collection, you will find half the fun is moving them around to create unique displays. Your tiny specimens become little works of art that bring life to unexpected spaces. Tuck them into small nooks where other plants will not fit and create ever-changing plant groupings and displays with abandon.

I collect many unique specimens and ephemera from nature, vintage glass, dishware, and of course many, many plants. Mixing my tiny plants with other objects from my quirky nature collection is hard to resist. Other than large furniture pieces, nothing in my indoor spaces stays in the same place for long. I am always moving things around and staging different items together to create interesting vignettes.

Sometimes, choosing an unexpected growing vessel or container for your tiny plant is all you need to step up your botanical style. While good old-fashioned terra cotta or mass-produced ceramic pots certainly offer both functionality and their own distinct style, I prefer to seek out unusual handmade pottery from individual artists for my tiny plant specimens. In fact, sometimes my tiny plants are a great excuse to acquire artful pottery.

Repurposing vintage glassware, kitchen canisters, teacups, or any unusual vessel to hold tiny plants is also a great way to stretch your budget and express your planty personality.

↑ A unique handmade planter is the perfect stage for your tiny plant.

→ Tiny plants allow you to create beautiful botanical tablescapes. If you sit down to dinner at my house, be prepared to share the table with a few tiny leafy friends.

↑ My favorite way to display my tiny plants is in fun vintage glass vessels. My mushroom canister collection might be a *tiny* bit out of control!

While some tiny plants may have a permanent home in a terrarium or large case, you can move around potted specimens to set up attractive temporary groupings. Use small glass vessels as mobile Wardian cases or glass canisters for high-humidity plants. Doing so gives you the ability to show off blooming or unique specimens, both for your own pleasure and for interested guests.

When moving tiny plants around for display, take care not to leave them in places where they do not receive enough light or humidity for too long. If a given species needs to be under a grow light in a naturally dark home, it is ok to move it to a more prominent display location for a few days or so, then pop it back under its grow light.

When displaying your tiny plants, think about creating combinations with varying heights and dimension. There are certainly many products you can buy to display plants, such as traditional platforms and risers made especially for displaying bonsai specimens or knickknack displays. That said, just about any household object can be repurposed to feature special specimens. Saucers, coasters, overturned glasses or plant pots, canning jars—all work like a charm. Stacks of books or clear acrylic boxes make the perfect risers. The lazy-Susan in your kitchen makes a fun rotating display stand. The options are endless.

How about planted furniture? You can find many new plantable furniture options these days, such as terrarium coffee tables and side tables. These fixtures act as glass cases or open planted vessels for your plants.

First and foremost, consider the light level where you plan to place a planted coffee table or other plantable furniture. If you position a planted coffee or side table in the middle of your living room, chances are the plants inside will receive low to very low light volume, depending on exposure, how many windows you have, and how far away your fixture is from the windows.

For permanent locations, always match plant to light levels or be prepared to add grow lights. If you place your vessel or planted table (with no grow light) in the center of a room, choose low- or very low-light plants. If you can place the planted table or vessel in a bright southern window or can illuminate it with grow lights, then you can include medium to high-light loving plants.

This is *not* a fairy gardening book by any means, but that does not mean you won't find me tucking in tiny pieces of décor, rocks and shells, or other collectables with my tiny plants or inside glass cases or terrariums. If you meet the environmental needs of the plant species, there are no design rules. Have fun with your own sense of botanical style.

↑ One of my nicer handmade Wardian cases holds some of my potted sinningia and African violets in bloom and on display under glass.

↖ A few of my tiny ferns, which I keep in a variety of glass jars, make lovely table centerpieces.

↑ Display tiny plants on bookshelves with other collectibles, but make sure to rotate plants back to ideal light conditions before they show signs of stress. Or, install low-profile LED grow lamp bars in shelving.

↑ A glass-topped side table, built for direct planting with a drainage valve, houses a variety of small succulents. You can also set potted plants into such planters and camouflage the pots with rocks or crushed glass.

→ Be sure to place planted tables or other vessels where they will get enough natural light or under grow lights.

↑ I display a group of living stones, *Lithops* spp., on my sideboard for a few days at a time; I then rotate them back to their grow lights.

← A teeny tiny brass treehouse and ladder look adorable as tiny potted plant companions.

OPPSOITE PAGE: My little zen garden is a stress reliever and the perfect spot for tiny plants.

conclusion

I **HOPE YOU** have discovered some exciting new tiny plants and are inspired to grow big collections . . . in tiny spaces!

Once you delve into the world of tiny plant species, you may have to hunt a bit harder than usual for your desired acquisition. While larger tropical houseplants are typically available in abundance, acquiring tiny species takes more time and effort. As with fashion, plant popularity trends come and go and what used to be in great supply may now be limited, or vice versa. I have a long list of tiny plant specimens I've yet to be able to find or acquire. For me, the hunt for the unusual is at the heart of a treasured collection. I see some tiny plant swaps in our future.

Once you begin *your* tiny plant journey, I am sure you will discover many more wonderful, itty-bitty houseplants to fill your home, and heart.

You can visit me online at **lesliehalleck.com** for my Plantgeek Chic blog and other gardening and horticulture information.

INSTAGRAM AND TWITTER: @lesliehalleck

FACEBOOK: facebook.com/HalleckHorticultural

FACEBOOK GROUPS: Plant Parenting and Gardening Under Lights

PINTEREST: pinterest.com/lesliehalleck

YOUTUBE: Leslie Halleck

LINKEDIN: linkedin.com/in/lesliehalleck

CONCLUSION

supply sources

Plants + Supplies

AIR PLANT SUPPLY CO.
air plants and accessories
airplantsupplyco.com

ANDY'S ORCHIDS
wide selection of micro orchids
andysorchids.com

BLACK JUNGLE TERRARIUM SUPPLY
exotic, rare, and unusual plants
blackjungleterrariumsupply.com

BLOOMIFY · *tiny terrariums and micro orchids*
bloomifytech.com

BUCE PLANTS
freshwater aquatic plants and accessories
Buceplant.com

CALIFORNIA CARNIVORES
wide selection of carnivorous plants
californiacarnivores.com

CARNIVOROUS PLANT NURSERY
wide variety of carnivorous plants and supplies
carnivorousplantnursery.com

FROGDADDY
specializes in rare terrarium and vivarium plants · frogdaddy.net

GLASS BOX TROPICALS
select terrarium plants and supplies
glassboxtropicals.com

GLASSHOUSE WORKS
rare and exotic hardy and tropical plants from around the world · glasshouseworks.com

IN SEARCH OF SMALL THINGS
rare terrarium plants
insearchofsmallthingsshop.com

JOSH'S FROGS
plants for terrariums and vivariums
joshsfrogs.com

LITTLE PRINCE OF OREGON
wide variety of succulents, air plants, and ferns
littleprince plants.com

LOGEE'S
wide variety of rare, fruiting, and tropical plants · logees.com

LYNDON LYON
African violets and companion plants
lyndonlyon.com

MICRO LANDSCAPE DESIGN
succulent seeds and plants, lithops
microlandscape design.com

MINIATURE GARDENING
miniature plants and supplies
miniature-gardening.com

MINIATURE GARDEN SHOPPE
miniature plants and supplies
miniaturegardenshoppe.com

MODERN AQUARIUM
live aquarium plants and equipment
modernaquarium.com

MOUNTAIN CREST GARDENS
large variety of succulents
mountaincrestgardens.com

SEATTLE ORCHID
large selection of collector micro orchids
seattleorchid.com

STEVE'S LEAVES
unusual and hard to find tropicals and houseplants · stevesleaves.com

THE VIOLET BARN
micro and miniature African violets and tropicals · violetbarn.com

Accessories, Grow Lights, Tools

BOTANOPIA · *cute accessories, propagation supplies for tiny plants* · botanopia.com

GARDENER'S SUPPLY COMPANY · *growing media, tools, grow lamps and shelves* gardeners.com

INNOQUEST, INC. · *quantum flux PAR meter* innoquestinc.com/product/spoton-quantum-par-light-meter/

LEADHEAD GLASS · *handmade Wardian cases and terrariums* · leadheadglass.com

MODERN SPROUT · *grow light bars, wall mounts, and hand tools* · modsprout.com

ORCHIDARIUM, LLC · *automated orchidariums* orchidarium.us

SOLTECH SOLUTIONS · *spotlight LED grow lights* · soltechsolutions.com

measuring light

As a professional horticulturist, I use a quantum flux meter to take accurate instantaneous Photosynthetic Photon Flux (PPF) measurements of Photosynthetically Active Radiation (PAR) from both natural and artificial light sources. I then quantify the accumulation of light volume over time. The accumulation of PAR—measured in $\mu mol/m^2/s$ (***not lux (lumens per m^2) or foot-candles***) over a 24-hour period—provides what we call a plant's Daily Light Integral (DLI), measured in $mol/m^2/d$. DLI is the most meaningful metric for understanding the amount of light plants need and how to deliver artificial light.

While natural sunlight levels outdoors vary widely throughout each day and season, you can estimate a PPF reading of 2,000 $\mu mol/m^2/s$ at noon on a sunny, cloudless day in summer. Over the course of the day, that could translate to a DLI of about 65 $mol/m^2/d$. Conversely, noon on a cloudy winter day may only measure 50 $\mu mol/m^2/s$ of instantaneous light; over the course of that cloudy day, DLI may only accumulate to about 1 $mol/m^2/d$.

You may be instructed to use a standard visual light meter, or a light meter on a smartphone, to provide lux or foot-candle readings for light in your space. You can do this if you do not need to get serious about light and simply want to ballpark general visual brightness categories. Using visual light meters is usually most useful for helping you realize how dim an area may be. However, know that lux (lumens) and foot-candles are not accurate measurements of light quality or volume needed for photosynthesis in plants. They are only relevant to general brightness categories for the human eye.

acknowledgments

I feel privileged to have the opportunity to write books and share my botanical passions with my readers. Privilege aside, writing and photographing books is a challenging and time-consuming endeavor. Especially during a pandemic. Creating a new book takes up all my free time, so I must first and always thank my incredibly understanding and patient husband, Sean Halleck. From occupying himself on weekends to ordering the take-out dinners to keeping my coffee and wine inventory deep, he is crucial to the entire process. Thanks, shmoopy.

Big hugs to my toddler nephew, Hayden Wiksveen, who FaceTime'd me almost every day for lunchtime together. You got me through, little buddy. Much love to my niece, his big sister Abby Wiksveen, for letting Hayden use her phone every day. Sorry we got so much yogurt on it!

I am not sure what I'd do in general without my account manager and horticulturist Jill Mullaney. She is my in-house book support team and juggler of all things in my business, Halleck Horticultural. Without her, I would not be able to both handle my business and write books. You are the BEST, Jill.

A nostalgic nod to the Luquillo Long-Term Ecological Research (LTER) program in Puerto Rico, especially Jill Thompson and Xiaoming Zou, who took me on all those years ago as an intern. I also cannot forget Joanne M. Sharpe, a modern-day renaissance woman, botanist, and fern researcher at LTER, who took me under her data-collecting wing. Without these fellow plant nerds, I would have never discovered that first tiny *Lepanthes* . . .

Much appreciation to everyone at Quarto and Cool Springs Press. Special thanks to acquisitions editor Jessica Walliser, who fortunately shared my enthusiasm for *Tiny Plants*, and art director Marissa Giambrone, who indulged my artistic quirks.

Gratitude to the growers and product vendors who indulge my constant quest for cool plants and tools, and who are always eager to work with me to help get them into the hands of my readers.

Finally, I must give my three tiny chihuahuas, Beezus, JoJo, and Jiggles, a special shout out as, apparently, they suffered gross and unendurable neglect on my part. At least that is their story. Don't worry girls, Mama's going to make it up to you!

about the author

LESLIE F. HALLECK is a Certified Professional Horticulturist (ASHS) who has spent her nearly-thirty-year career hybridizing horticulture science with home gardening consumer needs. Halleck earned a BS in Biology/Botany from the University of North Texas and an MS in Horticulture from Michigan State University. Halleck's professional experience is well rounded, with time spent in botanical field research, public gardens, landscape design and maintenance, garden writing, garden center retail, and horticulture and green industry consulting. At the end of 2012, Halleck devoted herself full-time to running her company, Halleck Horticultural, LLC, a horticulture industry consulting and marketing agency. Halleck is also currently an Instructor for the UCLA Extension Horticulture Program.

Halleck's previous positions include Director of Horticulture Research at the Dallas Arboretum and General Manager for North Haven Gardens (IGC) in Dallas, Texas. Halleck is now a regular feature on the professional speaking and industry publication circuit, but she also continues to offer up common-sense gardening advice and hands-on learning to home gardeners via her Plantgeek Chic blog, public workshops, plant swaps, and consumer publications. During her career, Halleck has written hundreds of articles for local, regional, and national publications, as well as taught countless gardening programs for the home houseplant keeper, indoor grower, flower gardener, edible enthusiast, and backyard farmer.

Halleck is the author of *Gardening Under Lights: The Complete Guide for Indoor Growers* (2018) and *Plant Parenting: Easy Ways to Make More Houseplants, Vegetables, and Flowers* (2019).

She is obsessed with all plants tiny and cute.

index